The Power of Your Inner Brilliance

Inner Brilliance
ACADEMY
GIVING YOURSELF PERMISSION TO SHINE!

The Power of Your Inner Brilliance
Stories of Self-Love, Self-Worth and Inner Confidence

DEBBIE BELNAVIS-BRIMBLE
with Seven Inspirational Female Experts

Published by Carnelian Moon Publishing

www.carnelianmoonpublishing.com

Editing by Dr. Malaika K. Singleton

Front cover design by Trevor Thomas

Back cover design by Simon Brimble

ISBN: 978-1-989707-00-5

Printed in the United States of America

Dedication

This book is dedicated to all women who pour themselves into nurturing, loving, inspiring, embracing, empowering, and supporting others to elevate in some way, including all the women who shared their journey for the reader's transformation.

To my mother, Heather, and grandmothers, Gloria and Clarice, and every woman around the globe—regardless of your age, ancestry, background, country of origin, beliefs, and experiences—may your inner brilliance be reignited as you reconnect to who you are truly meant to be, living your purpose, doing what you are passionate about, and embracing the infinite possibilities available to you always.

Contents

Preface

I never thought that my life would turn out like this. The many ups and downs have left me feeling so battered and bruised, yet I breathe hope and inspiration into the world and so do you.

How many times have your own words of encouragement lifted someone's spirits and left them filled with hope? I know there must have been many occasions if you are here reading this, seeking even more inspiration because you have so much more in life to give.

You are brilliant! You always have been, and you always will be. I say this as one brilliant woman to another. I would have doubted this fact years ago because although I am filled with hope and possibility now, life hasn't always been this way. I once had very little confidence, walking around hidden under a veil until my moment to truly shine arrived.

You probably have your own definition of inner brilliance and, as you read this book, I invite you to see your inner brilliance as *the diamond of your soul.* You have buried your diamond so deep inside of you, and you protect it fiercely because it is the most precious possession you have ever owned. It is this unique part of you, similar to your fingerprint, only you have this exact combination and design. It includes your purpose, passion, values, courage, confidence, resilience, personality, love, and so much more.

Every one of us entered this world as brilliant beings. The purest example of us displaying how we embrace our inner brilliance is as babies and very young children when they see their own reflection for the first time in a mirror. They light up with sheer joy at the brilliance that they see. There is so much magic in witnessing precious moments like that.

When I decided to write this book and invite other women to be a part of it, I carefully selected women who have had the most inspiring journey with many experiences, lessons learned, twists and turns, and their own secret sauce to success. The most important aspect of all our journeys is how we respond when we encounter challenges in life. As you read through the eight stories of women who are making a significant contribution to society today, I invite you to reflect on your own journey and see the road that you have traveled. Connect with the feelings of each experience you've had and acknowledge how you responded without judgment and with an open mind and heart to see, hear, and feel your own lessons of self-love, self-worth, and inner confidence.

Self-Love

Self-love is an unconditional deep sense of regard, appreciation, and acceptance for yourself on all levels: mind, body, spirit, and soul.

Although self-love is a very common term, it is often misunderstood and referred to in a narcissistic manner. In that erroneous perspective, those that practice self-love only care about themselves, love themselves at the expense of others, put themselves first, and don't care about who they hurt along their journey.

When we refer to self-love, we speak about breathing life into your own soul in a positive way, allowing you to feed others from your overflow. You cannot support others when you are going on empty yourself. The stories shared here are the personal experiences of amazingly powerful women who have ignited their inner brilliance with the power of self-love. In sharing their personal experiences, they are planting seeds of love for you to continue nurturing along your journey.

Self-Worth

Self-worth is having confidence in one's own value, worth, and respect.

Witnessing a woman who is fully engaged in her own self-worth is watching a woman who is in her full power. She knows who she is, her purpose, what she values, and what she wants. She values and respects herself and makes herself a priority in her own life. She knows how powerful her gifts are and that she is a valuable asset to her own life and the life of others.

The stories shared here are true authentic examples of women who have stepped powerfully into valuing themselves and knowing the true worth of who they are. May these stories give you hope in knowing that you too are invaluable and worth everything that your heart and soul desires.

Inner Confidence

Inner Confidence is having an unwavering, undeniable, unapologetic belief in oneself and one's abilities from the depths within one's soul and spirit.

Confidence as a whole is used on a daily basis, we all strive to be confident in our appearance, in our interactions, in our work, in our abilities, and how we show up daily in life. When we speak of inner confidence, we are thinking of confidence at such a deep level that we are focusing on the internal confidence that relates to who we truly are being on a daily basis. This confidence is not linked to what you own, what you have, the qualifications gained, the titles you hold, it relates to who you are deep within.

These stories of inner confidence by these courageously confident women have been shared to remind you that your own inner confidence is available to you, even when you feel that your inner power has been switched off or turned down. You have the permission to look deep inside of yourself and draw from your inner resources to support you in reconnecting with your inner power.

It is our intention for these stories to reignite your inner confidence, knowing that your inner power is available to you always, no matter the circumstances that you find yourself in. Look deep within.

This page is intentionally left blank

Replenishing Your Love Bank, The Amazing Powers of Self-Love

Isha B. Campbell

You may think you are alone, but trust me, you are not alone. Many of us were once slaves. Yes, I said it, slaves. I, too, was once enslaved and trapped in a world of guilt that was closing in on me too fast and it stifled me. But soon enough self-love surfaced and set me free!

The issue is, as women we tend to give everyone more of us than is needed or required. When it comes to taking care of ourselves, we are so overwhelmed and tired that we just put our dreams, wants, and desires on the back burner. We don't even take the time to watch our ideas and dreams brew. When self-love is missing, we tend to feel empty, resentful, and unhappy.

My definition of self-love is a deep awareness and balance of oneself as it relates to the acceptance of happiness that equates to having gratitude for one's overall life and the different accomplishments, relationships, and journeys along life's paths.

According to Merriam-Webster's definition of self-love, "it is a feeling of satisfaction that someone has in himself or herself and his or her own abilities." Now Google's definition states that "self-love is the regard for one's own well-being and happiness (chiefly considered as a desirable rather than narcissistic characteristic)." In addition, when you Google the word self-love and omit the word *definition*, it states that self-love is defined as "love of self" or "regard for one's own happiness or advantage" that has both been conceptualized as a basic necessity and as a moral flaw, akin to vanity and selfishness, synonymous with *amour propre,* conceit, conceitedness, egotism, and such (Wikipedia).

If you look closely at my definition of self-love, it sounds ideal. We should all have a feeling of satisfaction in ourselves and our abilities. However, pessimists in society, as usual, placed a negative connotation on the act of self-love. As a result, most of us now see it as a moral flaw associated with selfishness, egotism, conceitedness, and narcissism.

Studies have shown that conflicts will always exist over nature vs. nurture. Perhaps we were told, as a young child, by our parents that we are loved and therefore should love ourselves, but then nature (i.e. society) kicked in once we got older and told us we were being conceited and selfish when we showed any signs of self-love. So how do we align with nurture when society is constantly in our faces, everywhere we turn, telling us that self-love is a flaw associated with selfishness? The absence of self-love can make us feel depleted. Does nature have something to replenish our souls in the absence of self-love?

Putting the Pieces Together

When our backpacks of life are filled with unnecessary baggage, we have no room for self-love which is a necessity in our life. The lack of self-love creates an emptiness that pulls us away from living our lives to the fullest. We have no room to dream big nor the desire to create or even work on a plan of action to execute our dreams or ideas. In short, we are suffocated. The lack of self-love fosters broken relationships and creates a feeling of constant emptiness.

Core Solution

I recently had a family member send me a bible verse while I was in the middle of gathering my thoughts together to write this chapter, and as I read it, I saw how amazing God is in everything. I immediately saw how powerful love is. I opened the message and it said that "Love never gives up, never loses faith, is always hopeful, and endures through every circumstance," (*New Living Translation* 1 Corinthians 13:7). Think about it, our Heavenly Father is telling us that love is the key! And the most amazing and important aspect of this verse is that nothing about it states that this love was to be given or shown to everyone else, excluding ourselves.

So, what does this mean for us? Get reacquainted with yourself, go back to the beginning and start to learn about yourself. Practice some form of self-love every day. Why? Because it can ultimately get us to the next level in our lives where we begin to conquer our fears and grow into the amazingly brilliant individuals God created us to be. How amazing is that!

Never Lose Sight of Your Dreams

I remember when I started in my professional work role, I always had the desire to help people who were struggling in some capacity. I wasn't quite sure how I would go about doing it to make a living, let alone be happy doing it. I never created a plan to achieve it and when I did, it seemed so far from my reach. So, when I was hired by a new company, my dreams kept moving further and further away from me. I lived my dreams through the companies I worked for, making a niche for myself, but more so making that company a better place to work by fostering healthy relationships and by being that positive source of energy.

I would offer advice and kept nurturing coworkers and clients, but never replenishing my love bank. So, over the years I acquired this guilt that made me never look deeper into practicing self-love. My account was depleted. I was scared that even if I had the energy to give back to myself, I would be judged, even by friends and family as I also did the same for them . . . pouring out my energy. Over the years, my backpack of life became filled with mainly everyone's excess baggage. I made little to no deposits to my love bank and the few deposits I made were quickly withdrawn by guilt portrayed in nature: society making me feel that if I showed any ounce of self-love that meant I was selfish or as though I was better than everyone else.

What to Expect on Your Journey to Self-love

By the end of this chapter, I want you, the reader, to walk away seeing the rewards of self-love, self-care, and how when exhibited, your life will take on a whole new journey that pulls in this inner energy giving you a natural feeling of completeness and satisfaction—yes, you will begin to breathe again. This means never giving up on yourself by giving more to others than you give to yourself, never losing faith in yourself, therefore always being hopeful, and this gives you endurance through every single circumstance ... this, I believe, is God's ultimate desire for you.

My Journey Over the Years

Growing up in Jamaica, for about the first nine years of my life, I remembered seeing quite a few of my older family members married but living in separate countries for about six months of the year. One would be in the United States, Canada, or the UK while the other would be in Jamaica. As a child, I could never understand how that worked, and as a teenager, as I got to understand marriage and relationships, the thought of living apart from your spouse became even more complicated. Most happy couples I saw tended not to be happy once behind closed doors and I thought I never wanted any parts of this, and so I pushed away from marriage as to me it meant failure, especially after my parent's divorce. The thought of anything making me remotely happy like marriage had too many issues below the surface and so I saw self-love as a chore or an unimportant task in my already too long to-do list of life.

I just kept living life while comparing myself to individuals around me who seemed to be better off than me. I wanted to be successful but was fearful of trying due to my fears of failure and being judged. So, I buried myself into a mediocre lifestyle as this was safe and I would have nothing to be fearful of. I did just a little bit more than enough to get by, sometimes I would push myself but not very often to the next level as I was fearful of failure and felt guilty or didn't have the energy to give back to myself after giving and loving everyone else.

Fast forward years later after having children, purchasing my home, and graduating college, I was now sitting in a car facing a group of friends and family awaiting my arrival down the aisle. I remember my wedding day like it was yesterday; I remember having what I call a panic attack prior to stepping out of the car to walk down the aisle to say "I do" to a lifelong commitment to my soulmate and soon-to-be life partner. My chest tightened as I thought of what I was getting ready to do. Reality was sinking in and parts of my life were flashing before me. I remembered me saying in my head that I never wanted to get married . . . my reasons were, I simply never wanted to get a divorce nor live in two separate homes as that meant failure.

As I sat in the car, I thought about nature vs. nurture and I had to give in to one in order to pull through—it had to be nurture. You see, in my wedding vows, I revealed a very private feeling I had for years. I carried excess baggage around that kept me from depositing into my love bank. I felt that because I didn't live my life according to society's traditional order—I had children, purchased a home, graduated college, *then* got married—that I was somehow unworthy of my own self-love. I felt exhausted because I was always trying to play catch-up with those who lived life in the traditional order. So, I would focus on helping others, not knowing that if only I gave back to me, practice a little faith and just take baby steps towards self-love, things would just align themselves in the right order. You see, self-love removes those fears and gives you the motivation to push through your circumstances and be brilliant.

My wedding day was my major beginning to my baby steps toward faith and self-love. On my journey, I realized that to make this commitment work I had to practice more self-love. I started spending more time with myself and acknowledging my accomplishments, not holding them hostage. By no means was this easy. After years of pouring energy into others to make them see their self-worth, I lacked the energy to push myself. Although I knew my self-worth, my love bank was just empty.

Be Patient, Seek Guidance

Why do we, as women, practice the task of always pouring into others and not ourselves? Why do we think we have to save the world? Well, it's in our nature so we must learn balance. This is where self-love pushes us towards our inner brilliance. When our love bank is filled, we can make multiple withdrawals. Isn't this amazing?

I believe timing is everything; things don't happen in our time it happens in God's time. I remember when my love bank was starting to grow, I made some career changes to try something new, thinking this was going to change the way I felt about my job. It didn't work, my new journey with self-love made me hungry for more, and not just wanting to be an employee. I had always desired more but never had the energy to act on it. God said this is your time. I tried fighting it and remember a conversation I had with my mother-in-law about how do you know when God is talking to you. A friend of mine asked me that question and so I took the question to my mother-in-law. She advised me to tell my friend to read the story of Gideon in Judges chapter six where Gideon asked God for a sign. She went on to tell me that I should read it as well and ask God for a sign on what direction I needed to move with my professional life. You see, for years I wanted to open a clothing boutique to assist me with funding my foundation that would assist women deported to Jamaica in honor of late my sister, Donna.

Never Lose Sight, Never Give Up

Life kept getting the best of me. I failed to make deposits into my love bank and so my dreams went to the back burner and I was exhausted. I became discouraged because when I made steps towards fulfilling my dreams, something would come up and put me right back to square one. So, I questioned what my God-given talents were, and I questioned if I was to ever be successful or happy doing what I love to do. So, when my mother-in-law advised me to read the story of Gideon, I read it but fear took over. I was fearful to ask God to show me a sign if this was the right thing I was doing as it relates to my professional path and if my dreams were in alignment with his desires for me. Why? Because I didn't want to hear **no**.

So, months went by and I thought about asking God for a sign every day and even received some positive signs that made me deposit more into my love bank. Each day, I practiced self-love and grew into my comfort zone with loving me: yes, self-love with no feelings of guilt attached. One day, I gave in and prayed to God for a sign that will reveal to me my professional path. I prayed to him, asking if I was making the right decisions and if I was to continue with my dreams for my boutique and the Donna Marie Foundation. I received several forms of signs, so much so that it frightened me because I knew I could no longer stand still. So, at work, I decided that I would let the company work for me, I would no longer work for them in the sense of just pushing to be the best while making everyone happy and feeling good at work. So whatever trainings they had, I no longer saw it as a message on how to be better at work, I saw it as how can this benefit me in my own personal and professional life outside of work. That decision made work so much more tolerable as I now had a plan B with goals attached, a newfound meaning on my quest for freedom. I called my cousin and hired her as my life coach, which was one of the best life-altering decisions I have ever made. Again, depositing into my love bank, all in God's timing.

Life itself had started to inspire me. I have read so many motivational books over the years to keep afloat and nothing moved me like reading my cousin Debbie's book that she co-authored titled, *Women of Courage, Women of Destiny: Moving From Fear to Faith to Freedom.* Simply put, this book was amazing but most of all God allowed me to read it at the perfect time when I was ready to receive the message he had for me. You see, my love bank was filling up and I was now making consistent deposits as God wants us to practice self-love. I became more in tune with myself and my feelings. I no longer had the mindset of having my dreams sit on the sidelines, I was now ready to place them in motion. If we don't make it a habit to practice self-love with constant deposits, we take on too much baggage of others and don't have any room to receive our many blessings God promises us.

What I Love About My Life: Steps to a More Meaningful You

I love the positive direction my relationships are going in, my new business ventures, my relationship with God, and my new attitude on life.

1. Have a Dream, a Big One! My Dream

Before I even started working in corporate America, I wanted my own company. My dream is to be a philanthropist owning several companies worldwide to assist those less privileged. While working my many nine-to-five careers, I made it a point to learn as much as I could, both the positives and negatives of running a corporation so I could be well-educated on the ins and outs of business management. I worked as if it was my own company; I took advantage of every development and training that was available to me as I took pride in being the best version of myself at all times.

2. Find Your Support System

My support system begins with my relationship with my Jehovah. This relationship is filled with prayer, daily conversations, and faith. I also have my husband. He supports me. Our relationship is not just a marriage, it's a friendship, he is my best friend and life partner. I also have a very tight circle of family friends: my family who I consider my friends and my friends who I consider my family. I have learned over the years to keep this circle very small as this can become draining physically and emotionally if you don't replenish your love bank in the midst of this circle. You must know when to step outside of this circle to replenish and return; a good circle will appreciate and understand with no resentment or hidden agenda.

3. Be Bold in Your Actions

I always knew I didn't belong to the nine-to-five club. It wasn't my calling and so I have wanted to walk away from it the minute I started but didn't know how to. I felt trapped, I wanted to be able to spend more quality time with my family and enjoy life. I struggled for many years with a plan to achieve this dream. One day I got up and decided to take that leap of faith and so I prayed and received clear directions to call my cousin—a professional life coach—and hire her as my life coach. Getting a life coach has really changed me; I no longer have that guilt to live in my true brilliance in fear of what others may think. I now practice self-love with no fear of society placing a label of egotistical on me.

I have recently taken major steps towards practicing that self-love by stepping down and flipping it around so my life reads: full-time family member, entrepreneur, and part-time employee! I feel more comfortable with me stepping into my true brilliance with no guilt attached. I did it boldly! I am now the CEO and founder of the Donna Marie Foundation and its subsidiary, the Donna Marie Fashion Boutique.

4. Be Open to Possibilities

Each week, it seems a new business venture crosses my path and I can't tell you enough about how this is such an amazing feeling. If someone had told me, not even two years ago, that I was going to be an author, I honestly wouldn't believe it. But here I am now, being a part of this amazing journey with a group of brilliant female authors inspiring women around the globe.

5. Release Limiting Beliefs

Sometimes, we are our own worst enemy. We place doubts in our minds and they subconsciously manifest throughout the course of our life. We create stumbling blocks and negative energy that limits us in living out our true brilliance. This is caused by too much fear and too little faith.

6. Trust in God and Have Faith, Even as Small as a Mustard Seed

Don't just pray and get up and walk away because you will miss his reply—sit, be still, and listen. I, along with the assistance of friends and family, put on a *Talent for Charity* event—which will become an annual event—that was nothing short of amazing for my first major event outside my home.

Financial challenges were one of the hardest things I have had to overcome because I was a single mother that had to juggle work, school, and children for a long time. When I got married, it was a bit difficult as I was used to wearing the pants in the family and so letting someone in to assist and letting my husband play his role was hard. It was hard because, as women, we can lose our femininity in some relationships. When we are accustomed to doing everything, we place ourselves on the back burner again and find it hard to allow someone to take care of us because we have been doing it all for such a long time. We become hardened by society and find it difficult to replenish our love bank which can be, in some respects, a feminine part of us.

I have had to overcome the challenge of control, fear, and limited faith. You see, I would pray but worry. I would pray and not allow God to fix it; I would always try to control the outcome of my prayers by not relying on God's promises. I would forget that I was now married, and my husband made a promise to God to always love me, take care of me, and protect me. I had to learn to let go of my fears and take my faith to the next level, put God to the test. My father always told me to be specific in my prayers and my adoptive grandmother always reminds me that God promises to give us the desires of our hearts and so why should I be fearful, where was my faith?

Believing in My Inner Power

Along my journey, I had to be in constant prayer and be in tune with myself. I had to stand still and listen to God, listen to my body, and the universe which is all a part of practicing self-love. Once I got into the flow, things just started happening for me, I felt a path being paved for me. My love bank was now overflowing. As the songwriter, Jabez, says, "I'm drinking from my saucer 'cause my cup has overflowed!"

See, in life, we must have challenges; these challenges become our testimony to help and guide others along the way. No one gets to the top of the mountain when it's smooth. The bumps along the way give us something to hold on to; these bumps provide aid in getting further to the top of the mountain. So, too, in life these bumps are needed to get us to the next level which will eventually get us to the top.

Lessons Learned in Self-love

I have learned to embrace my challenges, then learn my lesson and move on. The time and energy we spend focusing on stumbling blocks deplete our love bank, therefore, taking us 12 steps back from our inner brilliance and our true selves. I realize that I can no longer focus on the past and the setbacks, I have to push through, pray, make decisions, and act on them. I keep picking myself up, acknowledging my so-called failures, and quickly moving on and not dwelling on them. Sometimes, at any given moment, I just have to push myself through and not wait on a divine motivation because I have it in me. God placed that brilliance inside each and every one of us, however, we get caught up and too bogged down with others' excess baggage that we lose sight of our dreams and God's promises for us to be the head and not the tail.

This is my calling, to be able to help women is my God-given gift and I can't afford to fight against it. Doing what I love and was called to do gives me natural energy, it replenishes my soul, it fills my voids which explains my feelings of emptiness while working to build other companies rather than my own.

I live life with no regrets because the path I took in life gives me a greater appreciation for what I have accomplished and the blessings I have yet to gain. We are all on an individual path to greatness and God makes no mistakes, so our courses in life are no accident—only a requirement to build upon for our next lessons in life. I have learned to embrace every choice I have made in life because in some way they have all assisted in my quest to living in my brilliance.

Each of us has a purpose in life; some of us have yet to figure out what that purpose is while others struggle to figure it out. The ones that know their purpose struggle to execute it while others struggle to find it in the first place. I have come to realize that when we tap into ourselves, pouring in self-love, our purpose and paths to achieve it becomes clear and our journey becomes rewarding.

About Isha B. Campbell

Isha is the founder and CEO of the Donna Marie Foundation and the Donna Marie Fashion Boutique, a nonprofit entity catering to the needs of deported women and children. She is a proud wife and mother who loves cooking and enjoys spending quality time with her family.

Isha is proud to be a philanthropist and currently assists women in the US and Jamaica who are in need of career guidance assistance, including resume building, mock interviews, and the donation of one set of interview attire.

Her aim for the growing foundation is to provide preventative support by becoming involved in visiting communities to educate them on the impact of deportation and the role it plays in the displacement of families, thereby breaking down those impacted families and the wider communities.

The Donna Marie Foundation has been a lifelong dream in the making and is very dear to her heart due to her late sister's deportation. Being deported from the country one considered to be home—where family is, where one grew up in many cases, where life is—feels like losing everything. It is especially disorienting at first, when everything feels foreign and overwhelming. There is no question that this is an even more severe ordeal for women, who are among the most vulnerable. The Donna Marie Foundation was established as a social intervention for women deported to Jamaica, aimed at providing them with basic needs—food, shelter, and clothing—for surviving, at no cost to them, for up to one year. Each year, over 350 women are deported to Jamaica from countries all over the globe. A large number of these women, having nowhere to call home once they arrive, end up homeless and become victims of abuse. No stranger to this injustice, the Donna Marie Fashion Boutique is an affiliate of the Donna Marie Foundation which is a non-profit organization founded in 2009 and named in remembrance of the late Donna Marie Belnavis, who died some years after she was deported to Jamaica in 1997.

We have a dream to provide a smoother transition for deported women. Our goal is to sponsor up to 20 women each year, giving them the opportunity to be self-resilient citizens, by providing personal and professional empowerment workshops, assisting them with resumes, mock interviews, and self-esteem building seminars.

We collect new and or gently worn women's and children's clothing, shoes, and accessories along with wrapped or unwrapped pennies. If you would like to give, but do not have the above items, consider giving a cash donation. Your donations will go towards building our first housing facility for these women. You can donate directly by clicking on the *donate* button on the Donna Marie Foundation Website - donnamariefoundation.org.

It is through generous donations like yours that the foundation will be able to provide life-changing experiences to thousands of women, and families by extension. Accept our sincere thanks in advance.

Isha holds a bachelor's degree in organizational development leadership psychology, from Saint Joseph's University, in Philadelphia, Pennsylvania. She has worked in various non-profit organizations that have a focus on behavioral health. She has over 10 years of experience working in the airline industry. She has also worked for WES Corporation where she created their first annual *Inside Out* self-esteem fashion show, which gave the clients the opportunity to participate in a five-week focus group that she facilitated, giving them techniques in building the whole person from the inside out to enable them to create a better version of themselves.

Fueled by an unquenchable passion for service, Isha has dedicated most of her life to serving people. As well as her Donna Marie Foundation, she is also an author and motivational speaker.

Donna Marie Foundation and Fashion Boutique

Website: www.donnamariefoundation.org
Facebook: Donna Marie Foundation
Instagram: DMFcharity and Donnamariebtq

Discovering Your Inner Brilliance Through the Art of Listening

Winifred Adams

Standing Up Again

It was a hot summer day just outside Fresno, California and I was lucky to be standing in the shade, readying myself to sing the national anthem to a stadium of excited baseball fans. I knew there would be a delay; I'd done it before. When I sang it for the Colorado Rockies on opening day, I was so excited and nervous but made my way through the delay in the stadium without a hitch.

But the day in Fresno was a different story. I began confidently, registering the delay and feeling the audience. They wanted me to succeed. They wanted to share in the inspiration I was leading, and then it happened. I tripped on a word. It wasn't the pitch, I missed my timing and the delay set me back, only now I couldn't make up the difference. I was lost and they were defeated. I let them down; and no different than an ashamed player leaving the field, I left, head down, a zero.

I have been known for my anthems. I've sung them for major league baseball many times. I sang them with great inspiration for drag car races, motor cross, ice hockey games, and at other odd events. I left them cheering with "tingles" as I was often told. However, this time in Fresno, I missed my mark.

As a bona fide athlete growing up, I was used to competition and even the agony of defeat on an otherwise good day; I knew that we as people have our ups and downs. The only thing that really defines an Olympiad or an Ironman contender from the hobbyist is the degree of dedication toward performance and the ability to rise again no matter the defeat. That ability takes both training and perseverance.

Athleticism came naturally to me—almost too naturally. In some ways, I took for granted my easy wins in swimming and my record-setting sprints. I just needed to add more fuel and pressure and suddenly things went faster. Only with singing, this absolutely does not prove true. You cannot apply more pressure to do better, lest you cut off your vocal cords and lose all of your sound. Instead, you need to relax more, hold your position, and keep your mindset solid. This is actually true of athleticism too. Think of the Kenyan and Ethiopian runners who more often than not, win the BOLDERBoulder and countless other marathons—barefoot—by automatically attuning themselves to a zen mode, whereby their bodies shift into a relaxed biorhythm, giving them strength and stamina.

Once I left the field in Fresno, I was embarrassed and honestly just simply confused as to how I could have done that. I didn't even finish the song it was so bad! Letting people down on their hard-earned ticket was worse.

Inner Drive

Yet, inside me was that natural-born athlete and I was determined to rise again and make it even better! A few weeks later, I was headed to San Francisco to audition for the Oakland Athletics—aka the Oakland A's. The stadium was empty except for a few of the people working the field and the person directing the microphone for me. On this warm, spring day I was eager to make this right. I got up, stood on home plate, and sang a cappella, letting the melody and words erupt as they always have, building to the end.

Stadiums are so dead in sound. My favorite places to sing the national anthem are ice hockey arenas where the warmth of bodies makes for a beautiful sound in the closed arenas, against the cold ice underneath my feet as I sing it.

This day in Oakland, I navigated the song well and was certain it was a shoo-in. That was until the woman with an earbud appeared to tell me someone high in the box said no, it wasn't good enough and I was to leave!

I burst into tears and literally cried the whole ride home to Fresno. This couldn't really be happening. What had gone wrong? What was the reasoning behind the no? I was given none. I questioned myself and relived the moment again and again in my mind. I was doubly defeated; no, I was crushed.

To put this into perspective, if I were told my audition wasn't chosen for the Grammy's live performance, that would be one reason to cry, but missing out on singing the national anthem for major league baseball was not really a reason to cry. It just wasn't.

I licked my wounds and put salve on my bruised ego, still wondering why they didn't think it was good enough. But I knew that answer would never come, and those people would have just as easily forgotten me that night when they went home as the rest of the lot who also didn't make it. It was then, I learned, sometimes you just aren't what they are looking for at that moment, and that is ok.

Witnessing Spirit in All

Fast forward a year or two later and there I was standing on home plate in Shea Stadium on a muggy summer day. This time the stakes were high. Here I stood in the very same stadium in which history was made over and over, both by major league athletes and, of course, the Beatles. Realizing that some decades prior, the Beatles changed history only a few hundred yards from where I stood, changing the game forever on stadium concerts and rock and roll!

These people of New York City were there to not only cheer on their favorite team but, as I soon would learn, for a heartfelt gathering of camaraderie. Their hearts were wary collectively, as they were still wounded from 9/11 and more recently a jetliner that blew up off the coast of Long Island without identified cause. The collective nerve was raw and the feeling almost tangible. Only, this time I was not there to sing the national anthem. I was going to sing "God Bless America" on Saturday, September 20, 2003, at the top of the seventh inning.

I was ready. I was in super shape and super mindset. And I had just gotten the insight regarding the effect on the people of the airliner explosion not long before. Somehow, I really could feel this as I took my position on home plate.

As I looked up, I saw myself front and center on the giant screen across the Shea Stadium field. Because of the delay, I decide to look to the right of the screen so I wouldn't see myself on the screen. I took my position and l lowered myself slightly as sometimes I begin to tremble more from the amount of energy that runs through me, than the nervousness of singing.

Slowly and deliberately I entered the song, hanging on the meaning of the words, and building to the first tier.

"God bless America
Land that I love
Stand beside her and guide her
Through the night with the light from above"

Then building into the next verse:

"From the mountains to the prairies
To the oceans white with foam
God Bless America
My home, sweet home . . . "

It was at this point in the song that I realized something awe-inspiring was happening. As I gazed out at the audience while feeling the words, ignoring the delay, I could see an enormous white light halo over the people at whom I was staring.

It began as a light halo and then began to get bigger and bigger like a rolling wave. Taken by this, I followed it and while singing, pivoted and began to turn to watch this light growing to encompass all of the people in the stadium!

Simultaneously, I was nearing the crescendo and people were clearly feeling what I was seeing before me. They were on their feet roaring and cheering in such a manner that was not common. By the time I hit the biggest part of the song,

"God Bless America
God Bless America
God Bless America
My home, sweet home . . . "

I hit the peak and ended on the sweet note of home, speechless. I stood there for a second looking around, taking in the energy of the people who were on their feet cheering, and at that moment, I knew something truly extraordinary had just taken place.

Humility

I had seen the souls of every one of the people in that stadium and they could simultaneously feel their own collective energy and blessing that seemed to come to them from on high! I got to be the witness to this unbelievable event.

People reached out to me as I passed by, grabbing my arms, saying thank you, both men and women, in tears. People stopped me in the halls and told me what that meant to them. I took it all in and was so grateful to get to be a part of that moment, and my heart swelled.

Now, just for the record I heard that—dead in the mic—recording later and I assure you it was ok but nothing of what it produced and invoked in those people! It was then that I knew something much greater than all of us, had touched us. It was a moment of hope and remembrance to all of the spirits in that stadium that day. It has never left me.

The simplicity of "God Bless America" is what makes this story so beautiful. It's not complicated, but rather, a heartfelt and meaningful song. And it was then that the people's hearts yearned for hope in a world so chaotic, without answers. That day in Shea Stadium, I was allowed to contribute my take on this magical song, and I was used to impart that hope from on high. How the light traveled across the people was so marvelous it is a wonder I could keep singing! I've never seen anything like that since.

In the Beginning

As a teenager, growing up in a conservative small town in Upstate, New York, we only dreamed of things we saw on TV. I always dreamed of singing but had no idea how one would get *there.* In high school, the girl who sat next to me in choir had just come from a competition against Mariah Carey, from New York! To us, that was *way over there.*

I was obsessed with fashion photography, modeling, make-up, and design. It captured my attention each week as I watched MTV and awaited Elsa Clinch on TV, sharing the latest in high fashion. Something in that world and the world of music had me captivated and I didn't quite know what that was, but I knew I wanted to be a part of it.

I set out to become a model. I was thin enough, fit enough, only not quite tall enough. They wanted you to be almost 6 feet tall and I was only 5'8 ½. My mother took me to New York and the agencies measured me and told me I'd only make it in certain levels of modeling such as commercial print. That was good enough for me! I'd take any area so long as it was doing modeling.

Soon I set a goal and just like in sports, I had my eye on the outcome—a contract to model. I spent the greater part of two years of my life preparing myself for my one shot. I'd improved my professional portfolio and set myself up to win.

The Unexpected

One day after school, I opened a letter telling me in fact that I finally achieved my long-earned goal and was offered an official modeling contract from American Model Management, in Spain! I was so excited! I jumped for joy and couldn't believe it! I was really going to do this! After sharing my good news with my parents, I was on cloud nine until my father walked into my room. He sat down on the end of my bed and said to me:

"You are not going to model and you are not going to Spain. You will go to college."

I protested immediately, "What? I can defer school for a year! I have to try."

My father looked at me almost in pity and said to me, "If you were so important, they would have found you and would have come to you, looking for you."

My brain swelled in my head and I felt like I was under ten feet of water. I was not really hearing this come from my father, was I? I was. I did.

He went on, "You will go to college, and there won't be another word about it." And he got up and left. He was right, there was never another word about it. I looked to my mother whom I felt betrayed me, and she sided with him, despite her cheering me on along the way.

Defeat

At first, the tears were non-existent and then they came in floods, in part because of the effort and the number of rejections I took for that one yes. But most of all, I felt sidelined by my father's coldness and his words. He never acknowledged that I had earned my way to a real legitimate contract.

Soon, my tears backed up on me and depression set in. I didn't want to talk to anyone, or see anyone, or do anything. I was lost. My soul felt crushed.

Modeling wasn't about beauty—it was about expression. Lighting, photography, and makeup all had a character element that I longed to try on, no different than emoting the words of a song. I never really forgave my father for those curt and unfeeling words he spoke. I came to understand that he didn't understand, but by then the damage was done. I'd never see me try at the agency in Europe and I'd never get the opportunity again. This was perhaps the most defeating blow of my young life. Parents never realize how passing words imprint into their children's energy field and psyche, but from my 20-plus years of being a professional medical intuitive/master healer, I've come to see how deeply the energy of words imprints into our nervous systems and cellular tissue.

Taking Back My Power

So, I deferred school anyway, and I went silent for six months. I wrote poetry and got it published worldwide and read the entire local library on metaphysics trying to find meaning to the things I intuitively understood or knew. It was a deep dive into a world of spirituality that I'd never been exposed to in my small town. This proved very meaningful to me and was the beginning of my healing work that has helped countless people across the world.

It would take me a few years to realize my better contribution to the world would come through my voice. Finding my voice was the greatest gift I ever discovered. Both my singing and my speaking voice were important but finding my inner voice and listening without reservation has since allowed me to help so many others because I can hear, not because I can speak. Dr. Scott Martin, my vocal coach, said something very valuable to me. He said, "If all the birds in the forest sounded the same, there would be no harmony." Those are some of the most profound words I have ever heard in my life. I have continued to contemplate those words and take to heart their meaning ever since!

And he was right. I didn't fit the norm. I never had, but I had no one to tell me that. I was a record-breaking athlete in both track and swimming. I was an achiever by all accounts and I really didn't know how not to be. My ideology was: you can, so you do.

Revaluing Truth

Yet, as I matured, I learned valuable lessons in service, deriving my reward from helping others. In my early 20s, I was lucky enough to find a living master—an enlightened teacher. She was gracious, and I learned by contemplating her words and by her extraordinary example. She told me, "Competition leads to stagnation and waste; cooperation leads to prosperity for all."—JLL.

Just because I can did not always mean I did from this point forward. Instead, I took to contemplating things first—as best I knew how—allowing myself to try on a different approach to my behavior in the world. This gave me a bigger perspective and eventually more choices, but more power to choose correctly.

The pain of the past with my modeling contract lingered but eventually gave way to deeper insight. I was not my one hard-earned opportunity, but rather I was what I *be* now. I learned that by allowing *now*, I was embracing the next opportunity and adventure.

Going to college after being silent for almost a year was an adventure and almost felt overwhelming to me. I did my fair share of youthful partying, but it was not really where I wanted to be. I wanted to be in the world expressing, inventing, working, and discovering. True to my Sagittarian nature, I wanted to be *doing* it! Yet, the discipline of school and the new adventure did teach me about the world and how to manage in it. For this I was grateful.

Finding My Voice by Listening

From those hard-earned lessons and setbacks, I not only went on to find my voice but blend my unique God-given healing gifts with my voice and now I produce a radio show, *Making Life Brighter Radio,* that speaks to hundreds of thousands of people in over 160 different countries. I have created and made music that has played in almost every single country on this planet and won both ASCAP and Billboard awards for my effort. I have created and made music videos and won an award for a video at the Zurich Film Festival. And more recently, I've been elected to be the vice president of the International Association of Medical Intuitives and published my first international bestseller, *The Silver Lining of Cancer*, along with 12 other courageous women. Next up will be my memoir, sharing my extraordinary and magical journey of life, despite the setbacks, and how following your inner voice leads you down a *yellow brick road of synchronicities*.

Life, I've learned, is all about your inner athlete. It's never about how you fall down, but always about how you return. Life is never about how you can't see, but rather how far you set your sight. Life is not about looking at another for comparison but looking at yourself with your eyes on your own plate, taking honest stock of what you find there and how to improve upon it. Life is not about the societal rhetoric, but instead, it is the beauty in being loving to the best of your ability, every moment of every day. Life is not conditioning—it's learning to unleash the authentic self from a conditioned self and polish that authentic self to a fine sparkle, your way.

Had I never failed I would have never dug deeper. And had I never been rejected; I'd never know my true inner strength. I've learned that people get excited for you when you do things they will never even try in their lifetime, whether you win or lose. This lesson was never more powerful than recently sitting next to an Asian gentleman at my local chapter for speakers, in Los Angeles. He was quiet and reserved until I asked him what he did. And it turns out he was the man most known for the worst audition for *American Idol*—William Hung!

This stunned me. It also naturally made us both laugh. Here he was, humbly sitting in a meeting as the rest of us, standing up and trying again. He was finding his new voice and realizing his additional talents, not his defeats.

How many times have we thought we were right only to find out there was more to learn? By spending so much quiet time exploring a subject matter after high school, I was able to enter the spiritual and healing world with many points of view which I could compare and sit with, including that which felt right to me. But most importantly, I learned to listen.

To hear your inner voice is perhaps the single greatest gift we can give ourselves. I've seen this countless times in healing. I even help people become aware of hearing the sound they inherently have within them all the time. Sometimes people think they have tinnitus, when in fact they don't realize they are hearing a preliminary sound of their own soul's voice! The aha discovery is so much fun to watch. Ultimately, each time someone really listens, they relax.

The Art of Listening

Learning to listen is hearing. And learning to hear is listening. In French, which ended up becoming my major in college, there are two words for listening. One word, *écouter* 'to listen to' and the other, *entendre* 'to hear' are used specifically based on the intention of the person speaking. In English, we intermix words, sliding around casually with our meaning. Yet, pilots that fly airplanes cannot say "right" without meaning "go right". "Right" as most of us would say, is changed to "correct" as a pilot, so as not to confuse anyone.

Today, we are bombarded mostly by our own thoughts. Learning to control our own thought processes has been my life study and my work with extreme healing. Redirecting or silencing thoughts is the key to healing and relaxation. **Thinking** about it comes to us naturally but **feeling it** does not. We value thinkers, thinking, and our own "I think …" thoughts. And none of that is listening.

The irony, I've found, is that when we listen to others and learn to listen to ourselves, we automatically discover our unique inner voice, guidance, and direction. It's the very inherent part of us that has been so easily trained away over time. And each time we come back to it we *feel more like ourselves*. We don't *think* more like ourselves, but rather *feel* more like ourselves.

My inner drive to be a model was my need to express myself in a family where I wasn't heard. My drive to sing was inherent in me. How and what I sang was a mix of my need to express myself, along with my inherent drive to move people by expression of music. So, what is driving you?

Is what's driving you inherent or conditioned? Is it learned, or from spirit? Is it taking you further, or setting you back?

Contemplation as a Tool

Contemplation has become one of the hardest-earned tools I've ever learned and certainly the most valuable. There are two types of contemplation, active and passive. For an active contemplation, you continually repeat that which you are contemplating, while sitting quietly until the brain shuts off entirely and insight comes along. Passive contemplation is something you carry with you while you are busy doing life and *mulling it over.*

These basic tools prove more valuable than any seminar and retreat of many words. What I've come to value most is the ability to glean profound insight from contemplation. Most people will not sit down long enough to endeavor to utilize these tools. They are merely a momentary fancy of effort. But, in fact they are a skill—an art form if used properly.

If I had only all that I know today when my father spoke those words to me. I didn't have a toolbox, and I didn't have any way to express myself. I was, instead, muted. That was then.

Success

Now I have my voice, inside and out! And I help people learn to hear their voice too! The best part is that my radio show has given strength to my word, my purpose, and my impact. But, if I never spoke another word, at least I'd know how to listen.

Go Jolly, W~

About Winifred Adams

Winifred Adams is a master healer with over 20 years of experience in body system health, biomechanical balancing, and emotional/physical trauma. An expert in Extreme Healing™, Winifred now shares her innate and rare gifts of intuition with audiences, creating an experience of Live-Time Healing™.

With the ability to see the origin of energetic imbalances, Winifred is considered an expert in her field of medical intuition and is one of very few people in the world who also has the ability to exact miraculous healing. Winifred's rare, but vast skill set shifts energy in Live-Time™, creating an environment for perfect and often complete healing. Winifred is the vice president of the International Association of Medical Intuitives.

With 20-plus years studying under a competent living master, Winifred has advanced her consciousness to recognize the subtleties of the ego and how profoundly it affects mental perception and well-being. Her in-depth understanding of energy has her wowing audiences both large and small, from corporations to auditoriums alike.

Winifred Adams, owner of Making Life Brighter™, the personality behind *Making Life Brighter Radio*, and is an award-winning columnist. Winifred is a recognized singer/songwriter with songs on iTunes and almost every digital media outlet, worldwide, and is a Recording Academy member.

Winifred's talent and penchant for healing extends throughout all of her artwork including fine jewelry design using the energetics of natural gemstones for healing; Designs by Winifred™ is "Fine Jewelry with Meaning". Designs by Winifred™ incorporates both the meaning of stones and the esthetic of sacred geometry for collectible pieces.

Winifred is now the author of several books including her unbelievable memoir, *On The Road To Enlightenment,* featuring her unique healing gift since childhood and how that gift took her on a spiritual and healing journey as well as adventures unimaginable! International Best Seller, *The Silver Lining of Cancer,* and an Itty Bitty Book® are additional works by Winifred, in collaboration or in total, in 2019.

A member of the National Speakers Association (NSA), Greater Los Angeles Chapter (GLAC) and the Women Speakers Association, Winifred is a professional wellness speaker "Taking Mindfulness™ to the next level!"

Making Life Brighter
Facebook: Making Life Brighter
Website: www.makinglifebrighter.com

Winifred Adams Music
Facebook: Winifred Adams
Website: Music www.winifred.net

Designs by Winifred
Facebook: Designs by Winifred
Website: www.designsbywinifred.com

Waking Up to Your Self-Worth

A personal account as experienced by Laura Atyeo

Laura Atyeo

Freefall

It's noisy at 12,000 feet. Rounded clumps of clouds float in the horizon below us. The wind roars into and around me, cushioning my belly somewhat—barely—and the ripples of my jumpsuit rapidly fluttering; everything is moving too fast, including time. I plummet in a downwards trajectory to the earth below. I am 50 seconds and 6,000 feet away from connecting the worm in my belly in the plane—and nearly losing all bodily control—with a salient, hitherto unrealized, problem. This dose of fear is more than the natural response to an imminent skydive, far beyond a thrill-junky shot of daredevil audacity. This is utter dread; it has the stench of death.

At 8,000 feet above the ground, I've completed most of my drills correctly, other than a sign one of the two instructors—who were falling with me—made that didn't connect with anything. Fixated as I am on the altimeter and the clouds above us, I had failed to change the angle at my knees, as we were flying backward relative to the landing point. What a newb.

I hear the buzz of white noise and a cacophony of roaring waves through the air and every aural capillary. This is my second jump and certainly the least fun of the two.

The first had been a tandem ride, with a Red Devil no less, a fantastic Aussie guy who had returned from a tour of Afghanistan, and to whom jumping out of a plane with a hysterical woman strapped to him was a little light relief of a weekend. It delivered a bliss-like buzz that lasted two full days, a golden suffused haze of recollection and lingering joy. Seeing the sky that morning so perfectly blue and imagining myself one with it, I remembered why I had chosen to do this jump in the first place. It was hearing the story of a friend of a friend, a shy young woman, describing her travels around Australia in a modest way, but who lit up like a firework when she told of her skydive above the beautiful Brisbane beaches and urged us to experience this kind of ultimate joy too. The long-anticipated day had finally arrived and the wonder of the natural splendor of the beautiful blue sky that morning gave way to nervousness that built to mild panic at the airfield and to mortal terror as I looked out the air hatch—in my final moments—onto the beautiful blanket of countryside below, dangling as I was ignominiously from a hero's shoulders. But then, the moment of falling out of the plane to complete surrender—surrender of all fear, ever and anywhere, and in its place, pure excitement. 100% joy! Like every hilarious joke, every moment of gorgeous surprise and elation, every spark of meaningful connection slam into your mind and heart all at once and all you can do is yell, "YES!!"

The main difference between a tandem and a solo skydive is that you open your own parachute on solo dives. The ripcord is an essential part of the skydiving equipment; when it is pulled, the parachute's container is opened, releasing the spring-loaded pilot chute and opening the main parachute. Booking a solo skydive shortly after the tandem skydive seemed like the obvious next step, with the plan to learn more about the art of skydiving whilst experiencing that unbridled joy all over again. But that is not my experience this time. I have no idea where my ripcord is.

The plane was dark inside, I could only just make out the bare struts and rivets of the fuselage; the open hatch blindingly bright. The engine was roaring just below; its throbbing and buffeting made me swoon, even while crouched down low near the cockpit, transfixed by the light. The shadow of the lead instructor hovered over me, asking me if I'm ok—I think to myself, "No, not really". I heard myself shout, "Yes!" He didn't answer but checked my emergency chute again. My gut has no facility with words, but still, it spoke ardently to me of something that was very wrong. It very nearly told me in a way that would be utterly undeniable to all present.

I jumped anyway. Routine as it was by now to ignore my body's messages and my intuition. Standing at the hatchway, toes over the edge, hunched against the ferocious wind, I was between my two instructors who both took tight hold with both hands to the four tough, handle-like ridges of fabric tightly sewn into my jumpsuit at chest and hip height. I remembered well the warning that you must jump decisively if you want your instructors to be there with you as you fall; that to hesitate and hold back as they go, yanking you out, can and does cause jumpers to spin chaotically—down, alone and disoriented. I shout out, counting to three. We lean out, then in, and on three we jump together.

I'm at 6,500 feet now; time to deploy the parachute. Then comes a hammer blow to the head. Where is the ripcord? Which side is it on? How high up my back? What does it feel like? Maybe it's tucked into something? Scrambling wildly behind me, I can't find it. The ferocity of the wind is pinning my swatting arm uselessly to my back. Three more seconds of fumbling and I'm now at 6,000 feet. Time's up and I'm in a complete panic. With my eyes wide and wild, seeing only clouds, a white-out . . .

And then, from within the orange filter of the next few minutes—blood pulsing throughout my system, my heartbeat at maximum, the voluminous breaths, and the kidney-squirting adrenalin rush—I had space enough to consider, if erratically, that in all the training and preparation for this jump, I hadn't once practiced opening the parachute. I hadn't even figured out where the ripcord was. We had drilled the emergency procedure into us, which I'd faithfully rehearsed over and over. Not once had I envisioned success. An instructor pulled the cord for me.

The glide down was pleasant enough. I rolled out the emergency procedure once more on landing. I came in too steep and my shaking arms were unable to brake the chute fully as I careened into the ground at 30 mph or so. My chin was bloodied from biting it on impact. I gathered up the parachute and strode off the airfield. I was so proud of myself for taking that leap.

It is not unheard of, by any means, for instructors to help a skydiving student on their first solo jump to deploy the parachute. Nonetheless, it was a cold sweaty business contemplating the—as I perceived it—utter recklessness of my actions in not being prepared to carry out the jump successfully. Fear of what I had done and what it all meant clouded the empowering lesson and it took me many more years to see it.

Facing the Truth

Today I love who I am and how my life is right now. I am living a life-long dream of being a musician and I'm the founding director of a thriving social enterprise that serves by promoting engagement with music and the creative arts. I have a beautiful family, wonderful friends, and I live in a home and community that I love. Crucially, I have connected to my greatest strengths and talents, discovered my purpose in life, and I am living it.

It was not always this way. I spent much of my life—up until very recently—feeling stressed much of the time; a kind of palpable, ever-present, head-rattling tension around the head and neck. Worse than that, I carried heavy, painful feelings of shame, inadequacy, and dread from experiences in my past. I was otherwise healthy and intelligent. I had a fine career and lots of potential. I had the opportunity to be anything I wanted. "So why am I in this painful, fearful state?", I asked myself repeatedly. Why do I spend so much energy worrying about what others think, people-pleasing in order to gain small doses of approval, sacrificing my own authentic self in the process? I couldn't see what I truly desired in life—what would make me deeply fulfilled and joyful—something I could be so passionate about that I'd feel electrified and vital, knowing I was pursuing my dreams and, in doing so, contributing to others.

I had been living a lie. I gave extra time and effort in personal relationships, friendships, and in my career. However, the painful truth was that I often did this to bolster my own sense of self-worth and get a sense of approval and belonging, rather than for selfless, altruistic reasons and a genuine desire to see other people become happier and contribute to society. I was insecure and weak. I had a poor sense of self.

I was resentful and bitter towards people who hadn't reciprocated when I had given so much. I had hateful thoughts and fantasies of revenge that were sometimes all-consuming.

I gave myself the highest of standards to meet in punishingly short deadlines, then I'd sabotage my own efforts—as soon as I made some progress, I would undo it. Then I'd scold myself. And repeat the whole sorry cycle over and over. And I didn't understand why.

Today, even with all the achievements on my bio, I am not the finished article—although I do believe one never stops growing and learning—and not all of my goals have come to fruition yet. I still experience doubts and I can slip into old habits that disrupt my efforts to reach my heartfelt ambitions. I overanalyze and I chastise myself for mistakes—and worry about doing both often.

Throughout my journey, I had realizations along the way that are far more significant and powerful than any of my many shortcomings. I will share what I realized with you; however, the ultimate power lies in the meaning I gave my experiences and the choices I made as a result. My greatest hope is that, by the end of this chapter, you will be inspired to uncover your deepest desires—if you haven't already—and follow them.

The Well

There have been dark times. Pain in my heart so full I can't breathe. The muscles in my chest could barely release to let anything in, no room for anything else, not even air. Many times a day, my heart would flutter like a caged bird in my chest and only then would I draw a breath in. I stopped drinking water. I had an exit plan.

The pain was deep, throbbing, and reverberating. The thorns in my chest were tangled and interlocked. Attempts to wrest one strand free only served to pull the others tighter. Falling asleep was resigning myself to dreadful imaginings mingled with unbearable reality. I clung on to wakefulness—terrified of what I would see when I closed my eyes—desperately till, in sheer exhaustion, I lost my grip. Sleep was laid bare, with nothing between me and the shadows where unfettered horrors waited. In my dreams I see…

. . . the gaudy gilt-edged screen showcased a perfect microcosm. Bums on seats squirmed in crumby, grimy chairs—unkempt—rotten litter in the aisles and squelchy underfoot. A hiss of the gas lamps lining the theatre house—it was an old film. Out back where no one ever went tangling, thorny vines proliferated ...

By day, I functioned normally—doing well in my studies and holding down jobs competently—doing the usual things a twenty-year-old would do. I had friends and I socialized, laughed, drank, etc. What made this especially difficult was that I didn't recognize the feelings of hurt, shame, and guilt I was carrying and, even if I was dimly aware of them on some level, they made me feel disinclined to share my feelings with anyone else and so I isolated myself. I had just got out of a very destructive relationship and wanted some alone time. The result was that I had little meaningful contact with anyone for months, kept alone with my thoughts and crippling emotional pain until I gradually began to despair.

Lying in bed at night, I imagined how sweet it would be to go mad. I tried to forget everything, even my own name. I practiced diligently every night and was pleased when I asked myself what my name was, and I couldn't recall. But I could not ignore the pain in my body, and I could not forget. And that was when I planned to take my life because death no longer held any fear—it was an escape, a relief.

I'd hit the proverbial rock bottom. For me, it was a well with jagged rocks tight-walled around, so deep down that there was no light at all, only pain. All hope had fled, and I was tormented nightly with flashes of images that were so disturbing. Right at the bottom of that well—compounding it all—I felt the pain of others out there. All the suffering on the news from death, crime, and war seemed to shout out like shock waves that seared into my heart. The chaos and confusion blotted out the day and extinguished hope and light itself. I couldn't see a way out of the horror and despair.

My room was painted blue. Research notes were piled neatly on the desk and CDs lay scattered on the floor beside my little CD player. Opaque light gleamed through the net curtains at a large window; it was cloudy. My bed faced the desk and I caught my drawn face in the mirror, head sunk onto my chest, contemplating another disturbing night.

But then something stirred. A distant memory, misty from the years since. The feeling came first—warmth and thawing—a faint whisper of love. It was like a beautiful melody amid thrumming crowded noise. It came straight from my heart; the very place that had held so much pain started to sing a different tune. I just had to listen. What came to me then was the memory of a walk I took with my grandad when I was eight years old. I remember little of what he said but his avid presence on that day spoke volumes, and years later, I felt what he said: "I'm here for you. And I love you."

It was the one and only time I can recall it being just us two, my grandad and me. I had just started learning how to play the violin. Two boys at school agreed that I sounded like a donkey braying. I thought they were right. The sky was flat, gray, and nondescript. We were walking along familiar roads in a poky parochial town. But something woke up that day. I talked to him and asked questions I thought were boring and irrelevant, like what the triangle sign means at a road junction. And he explained like it was interesting and important.

He was present. He was someone I loved and admired and respected greatly. He listened. He was there with me. There was a powerful connection—like my heart was beating for a reason and my voice was being heard. The grayness above was charged with energy like an ignition. I had no idea at the time that this connection would save my life.

Alone at the bottom of the well, deep down inside me, there was love.

Living as My Authentic Self

Climbing up the slopes of the Long Mynd last year, picking through the coarse heather, I love the stillness, hearing nothing except ourselves and the music of the skylarks as they climb above us. Just me, John, and our two beautiful boys. We had a great morning in a local village hall, catching up with friends, joining in the drumming circle, and sharing lunch. Now we are walking together, seeking out a great spot for a rest and a picnic. Life is full. There is so much to enjoy and more to look forward to: orchestra practice—we're doing Tchaikovsky's fifth—shaping my new business and musical services to the community, meeting new friends in our new hometown, and enjoying the colorful tranquility of our growing garden.

There's so much I love about my life right now. First and foremost, my family, my husband, and the love we share; being with my sons who are healthy, happy, and so creative and loving. Looking in their eyes, I see oneness, love, and intelligence beyond comprehension. Such a strong force of love that I am compelled to be present. They call to me to join them on the picnic rug, a wedding present when our eldest was on the way, giggling together as they lounge over the brush underfoot. John looks happy; he's relating another fell running adventure over the range opposite us as we look out towards Wales.

I haven't yet formed my business, but I know it's in the cards. I picked up the violin only a year ago after three decades, but I know I will be playing it with and for others before long. I had decided a few months previously to acknowledge what I had long felt was my true purpose but hadn't quite had the courage to speak it: that my purpose in life was to feel all the joy, adventure, color, and music of being alive and play and share it with others so they can experience that joy, fulfillment, and empowerment that comes with living your true purpose.

I remembered the stories of my life and the great gifts I have received. I knew that the greatest gift I can give to others is the one my grandad gave me—being present and connected. At last, the visions that once haunted me disappeared.

... the film had rerun for the last time, that gaudy light went out for good ...

Feeling all the beauty at that moment on the hill enjoying a simple family picnic, I didn't know for sure how I could make it all happen. But given all I have experienced, it is fantastic I am here at all in this state. I could have ended my life; I could have made a different choice. Being here and being in this beautiful state is my choice. And I feel so powerful. I will find a way to make my vision for my life a reality.

Pulling My Own Ripcord

Life was very painful before I started to acknowledge my self-worth and make the necessary changes to live in a more authentic way because I wasn't being true to myself. I regularly ignored my own intuition and I frequently put aside my own values of love, courage, and authenticity. I sacrificed my integrity, peace of mind, and many healthy relationships in order to achieve and gain approval—often from people who did not value me.

It seemed like there was a mountain to face when I set about the problem of how to undo years of habitual worry and tension. But it turns out that the steps to success were a lot simpler than I thought because these steps were defined by my experiences and my decision to honor the truth of who I am.

I believe we are shaping our own destinies by continually choosing between either love or fear. I chose love—and I feel that that experience I had with my granddad when I was eight years old decided the course of my life more powerfully than I could comprehend for many years.

Starting from low energy and no precedent is the hardest. What started the momentum for me was practicing gratitude meditation, ten minutes every morning. Simply taking a moment out of the day—before I got caught up with life's demands—to focus on and feel the love and gratitude for different experiences in my life, big or small, very quickly made a big difference. The power lay in deciding to shift my attention: to dwell on those moments that I could be grateful for with the same intensity and curiosity as if they were one of the many seemingly intractable problems I habitually focused on.

I thought about a moment of love, joy, or wonder—something recent or that happened long ago —and allowed that feeling of deep gratitude to form in my heart. I then thought of two or three more such moments and allowed that feeling to grow. When in that beautiful state of mind and feeling, everything in my life was transformed. I saw beauty and joy in so many things. Even deeply painful experiences became amazing lessons when I could see and feel my own personal growth from them. And I started to recall experiences that I hadn't thought about in a long time but that had deep and positive meanings for how I have become the person I am.

The other big change I made was to honor myself by feeling my feelings. By that I mean, processing and releasing all my feelings, even the ones I wished were not there, by simply feeling them and letting them play out. The healing was particularly powerful in relation to feeling and releasing the more vulnerable emotions of sadness and grief.

As weeks and months went on, practicing feeling grateful and honoring my feelings every day, quality time and space began to open up for me. I had more moments of clarity that enabled me to see the beauty of the present moment. I could now allow myself to feel grateful and abundant for all I had. Living this way, I truly value myself.

There is Always a Way

The biggest lesson I have learned is that love and purpose are paramount. From my experience at 6,000 feet up, I learned that my life and happiness is my responsibility and mine alone. No matter what challenges I face, assigning blame is a waste of precious time and energy. I alone am accountable for the quality of my life.

Even at the bottom of the well, I had a profound feeling of what it is to love even when hope seemed forever extinguished. As a result of this, I believe love is to be found everywhere and is a more powerful force than anything I know.

From living more authentically, and from knowing and loving my children, I finally realized that I must listen to my body and follow my intuition; the jump was a blatant clue.

I woke up fully when I realized the power of that moment with my grandad—the power of being present and loving unconditionally, and what that meant for my self-worth. He also played the violin and was a huge inspiration to me as it helped shape my purpose in life. I knew without a doubt that I was worthy and the significance of his gift to me.

The most abiding and powerful principle I learned in early childhood, perhaps in the very first years of life, is that *there is always a way.* I believe that anything in life that we sense, imagine, or experience directly can be recreated and represented in any way that we want. We create our own sense of meaning and purpose in life. So, make it empowering. Make it amazing and something you love.

I would say to you that your answers and greatest heartfelt desires are already within you if you look. Certainly, what worked for me was to jump in with both feet.

About Laura Atyeo

Laura is a musician, singer, writer, and founding director of Open Harmony CIC, a social enterprise (non-profit) company providing musical and creative arts services in her local community and across the region.

Our vision is a world where everyone experiences uplifting, life-changing moments where they feel connection, joy, and find purpose through music and creativity.

Open Harmony is all about creating uplifting, transforming, and joyful musical and creative art sessions with those in the community who will benefit most from the incredible therapeutic effects of live music and the arts—including song, poetry, drama, dance/movement, the spoken word, and visual arts. These sessions are inherently interactive, sensitive to the needs of the client or client groups, and flexible in order to enable clients to experience those spontaneous moments of joy, connection, and transcendence that spark newfound confidence and insight. We aim to have a hugely positive impact on the quality of life and well-being of everyone we serve.

Services include songwriting and music creation, forming and leading choirs, improvisation, directing performances, and enhanced well-being programs that aim to deliver greater health, well-being, and confidence over the longer term. At our sessions, you can expect a warm welcome, a safe, relaxing atmosphere for the creation of music/song/art with others; to have lots of fun, and perhaps to uncover hidden talents you never knew you had. Our services are universally accessible, regardless of experience or ability.

Listening to and participating in music can have a host of scientifically-backed benefits, including increased socialization (making new friends, strengthening relationships), improved mental and physical health (feeling vital and healthy, reduced pain and sleep problems), improved emotional well-being (feelings of happiness, relaxation, and reduced depression, anxiety, and stress) and strengthened learning and memory (improved outcomes for people living with dementia, children and young people, people recovering from surgery or strokes; the list goes on). Through being fully present, open, and working in harmony with our clients, our services aim to deliver all the benefits above.

Visit our website www.openharmony.co.uk for your free gift that we hope will inspire and share more insight into what we do.

The expected transformation: that each client is enabled to be happier, healthier, with a better quality of life, and more of who they want to be.

Open Harmony
Website: www.openharmony.co.uk
Facebook: Open Harmony Music
LinkedIn: Laura Atyeo

This page is intentionally left blank

A Brush with Change

Judith Richardson Schroeder

How a close call on a Northern Ontario highway changed my perspective about life and taught me how to experiment with yes!

The Road to Change

So often we walk through life not really noticing some of the most important moments unfolding around us throughout our days, or even being able to recall what made them important, special, or memorable. Sometimes, if we are lucky, we'll decide without too much convincing to begin to pay closer attention to the moments that are flashing by in life. To the special goals we've had and how we've planned to execute them or make them happen at all.

Then, one day, something wakes us up. It might be an illness or passing of a loved one or our own health challenges, or it could be something that really shakes us up, like a close call that brings us to the brink of realizing we aren't immortal, but perhaps we've not really been living our best life, and now, it seems more important than ever that we do.

Such is the experience I had on a cold dark night on a Northern Ontario road. I was not only shown how fleeting life really is, but I was also shown just how quickly something can happen to change the way I live now. I gratefully took away a learning moment from the experience, but I also discovered a unique way to set and achieve goals in such a way that I not only completed goals that were years overdue, but I achieved them with more ease than I had ever anticipated. If you've been struggling like I was to achieve some of your most important goals and aspirations, I'll share with you how I've overcome procrastination, achieved long-standing goals and continue to achieve my dreams today!

Delays Pave the Way for Gratitude

The rivets on the side of the bus were so close I could have reached out my window and touched them as they drifted by. The slow-motion of the passing bus seemed to match the slow-motion of my vehicle as we passed one another—mere inches between us. I was mesmerized, and oddly, although I should have been, I wasn't the least bit concerned!

We had left Edmonton, Alberta, on a cold, steel dull day just days before the New Year celebrations where to grip the country. Two of my children had driven my car out to Edmonton a year before, and now my husband and I were following each other home as he drove our second car back to Ontario with me following along in our two-month-old car.

The weather promised to remain overcast and snowy as we set out that morning for our long trek home. We had driven the 3,600 km (2,237 mi) stretch every year since our first visit in 2013. We loved the drive and tried to make it out to visit our three sons and daughter as often as we could. Now, we were headed back home to celebrate New Year's Eve and ring in 2015. But we didn't realize that weather and one of the vehicles wouldn't let us keep that schedule.

The first day's travel was relatively uneventful. The weather didn't cooperate much, but the snow, when it did fall, was light and barely accumulated. We pulled into Winnipeg, Manitoba for the night, staying at one of our go-to hotels, Motel 6. The bitter cold was already promising it would be a rough night, and we were grateful to have a warm place to spend it.

The next morning, the second day of our three-day trip dawned steely grey and bitterly cold! It had been one of the coldest nights on record in Winnipeg for a long time, and the temperature had plummeted to a bone-chilling -50 °C (-58 °F!)

My husband and I hopped into the cars, and as I started mine, I could see my husband looking over at me and shaking his head. My car had rolled over painfully slow, but then caught and came to life. My breath was creating mini clouds inside the vehicle, and as the GPS camera struggled to bring up the map, the screen began jumping, blurring, and flickering, then froze, done struggling to come to life in the bitter frost. I looked over at my husband still trying to start the other car, but I could tell there was no joy. We weren't going anywhere!

It was the 29th of December 2014, and we had to find a garage that was open that would be able to repair the car. Every towing company we called gave us the same report. The wait for service was several hours. By 2:00 p.m., a truck was on its way. Unfortunately, a boost didn't help, and the problem proved more severe than a battery boost could fix.

Three days passed before we found a garage able to order the part needed, and when it arrived, my husband shivered in the bitter cold as he worked to change the alternator on the car. Almost a week later, we began the second leg of our three-leg journey. With my husband leading, we said goodbye to Manitoba and headed into Northern Ontario's severe band of weather.

Death Drifts By and Divine Guidance Takes the Wheel

Snow squalls met us every few hundred kilometers. As we crossed into Ontario late that afternoon, the snow began to fall steadily, growing heavier in accumulation by the hour. By nightfall, we had traveled through blinding snow for over 11 hours while following a snaking line of traffic for most of it. My eyes were tired from concentrating heavily on the road ahead, but I was looking forward to getting off the road for another night.

This evening would be very different, however. We soon found ourselves sitting in a long line of traffic, stopped on a Northern Ontario road while word spreads that a severe accident had just happened ahead. Fifteen minutes later, we heard the wail of an ambulance siren coming toward us, and suddenly, it was speeding by us, lights flashing, sirens screaming. Almost 40-minutes later, the ambulance made its way back past us slowly, siren silent and lights flickering eerily. I don't think any of us on that stretch of road that night doubted what had happened. At least two people wouldn't be making it home to their family to ring in the New Year. The stark reality was palpable, and for many of the weary travelers that night, the journey would be made with a little more caution.

As the traffic began to move ahead slowly, we all gingerly drove by the collision site. A U-Haul five-ton truck lay on its side, crumpled and twisted far off the road in the ditch on one side of the highway. On the opposite side of the road lay the twisted log truck, its load strewn into the ditch and lying scattered around it. I felt my stomach drop, and in silent prayer, I mumbled, "Rise in peace." The line of cars ahead, including my husband directly in front of me, began to speed up now as we left the carnage behind. Suddenly, a pink and gray Greyhound bus on the other side of the road was edging toward the centerline obscured by inches of accumulated slush and snow.

My eyes caught the bus driver staring straight ahead, almost oblivious to the fact that he was hugging the center line more and more. But, before I realized it, my head was turning to look out my window, and I was caught up in the mesmerizing glint of the aluminum of the bus edging closer and closer to my car. The bus passed in full slow-motion style, and I felt as though my head was also moving in slow-motion as I watched the rivets on the side of the bus came closer and closer to my car, yet I felt no fear or concern.

I'm still not sure how or why, but as I stared at the bus edging just inches from my car's side mirror, something was guiding my hands on the steering wheel, because when I finally realized I needed to steer away from the bus and toward the ditch, I was finally able to look away, and as the bus flew by I found myself edged close to the ditch beside me.

My hands had turned the steering wheel away from the bus even as it continued to encroach on my side of the road. How I did not die that night is a mystery, but it was an encounter that forever changed my outlook on how I walk through life and how I honor every day that I am here on this incredible globe to enjoy, now.

By the time we reached Thunder Bay after midnight, I was ready to call it a day! The snow was deep and challenging to get through, but we had made it safe and sound to the hotel. As I closed my eyes that night, I wished for a day filled with sunshine and clear roads for the final day of our journey home.

Spared Again

The next morning my wish was granted, the sun shone brightly, and there was no sign of snow in the forecast. By mid-afternoon though, we once again found ourselves parked on the side of a road, waiting for an accident to be cleared. By now, I just wanted to be home safely in my bed, but we still had a full day journey, and safety was uppermost on my mind.

By 7:00 p.m., we were heading into territory that we knew well, into the home stretch just a few hours away from home. And the snow had begun falling again! It was a moist smattering of massive snowflakes at first, but quickly began to cover the road making it slick to drive on. Just before a small military town called Petawawa, my husband crossed a bridge, and suddenly the walkie-talkie came alive in the seat beside me.

I picked it up, "Yup?"

"Whatever you do, slow way down before that bridge. The cold must have buckled it or something, but I almost lost control when I went across it. So slow down and be careful!"

I'd gotten the message just in time as my front tires hit the edge of the bridge that had partially separated from its moorings, making the roadway dangerously uneven. The car slid slightly but stayed solid as I moved across the bridge to the other side. Just a few hours later, we would learn that someone crossing that same section of the highway would lose control and lose their life. This trip had been one of the most treacherous ones we'd ever experienced, and the lives taken on that trip was a sobering reminder that our life is indeed a moment by moment gift never to be taken for granted.

As we edged closer to home and the lights of the city, a long string of cars was coming the other way. The combination of Rain-X on the windshield and wipers and the constant onslaught of oncoming lights was making it difficult for me to see the road. By this time, I was so tired I just wanted to be off these crazy roads! The walkie-talkie woke again.

"Yup?"

"You might want to get closer to me so you can see where you are going more easily." My husband was worried I was trailing behind him too far.

"I'm good. I can't see well when I'm closer. I'll be fine."

"No, just pull up behind me."

"I'm tired; I can't see where I'm going, all these cars, what are they doing on the road this time of night anyway?"

"Hockey game. They're headed home from the game."

"Well, I'm done! I'm not pulling up, I'm not speeding up, I'm done!"

I threw the walkie-talkie onto the seat and continued squinting through the smeared windshield and oncoming glow of headlights, staring at the side of the road to gauge that I wasn't the one too close to the centerline now.

By the time we rolled into our driveway, I wanted to jump out of the car and kiss the ground, all three feet of snow and slush included! But, instead, I sat behind the wheel of the car and whispered, "Thank you!!! It is so good to be home safely!" Then, my thoughts went to the people who wouldn't be going home to loved ones, and I whispered another thank you for the divine hand that had guided us safely home and said, "Peace" under my breath as I opened the car door and stepped out of the car for what I hoped would be awhile.

Stepping Beyond the Comfort Zone

Once I settled into a routine again and I was busy doing life, I didn't think too often of that trip or the impactful events that had happened. I wasn't even aware that they had begun to work on me from the inside, from deep down in my subconscious where it mulled over the close call, time and again, often briefly bringing the vision of the slow-motion movement and how dangerously close the car had been to that bus. How near to death had I been? I didn't think about that much, but I did know that someone had been watching over me that night. There was no doubt about it.

Then, one morning in August 2016, I woke early from what seemed to be a dream where I was reliving certain parts of the trip, but nothing had been clearly evident. It was more a feeling than a knowing, but it had disturbed me and left me questioning what on earth was I doing with my life.

I came downstairs, made a cup of coffee, and went to sit at my desk in my home office. Before I knew it, the sun was shining, but I was still sitting there, staring out the windows. I'd concluded while sitting there that morning that I wanted more.

I'd taken a journey in my mind that had me viewing myself walking through life. Stopping to see everything I had accomplished along the way. What I noticed quite obviously was that I had a lot of unfinished goals. That surprised me because I had always been someone who set goals and went headlong into accomplishing them.

I recognized several goals I'd not yet fulfilled, and I made the decision that morning to change that. It seemed the moment I made that decision, the universe opened the doors and said, "Finally, let's go!"

I decided to experiment because being a subconscious behaviorist, I know a little about how the subconscious works and how it does its best to keep us safe and comfortable in our knowns, otherwise known as our comfort zone. I wanted to be sure I wasn't going to get caught and not move forward if I decided to step way out of my comfort zone. I needed a list of parameters to help me achieve my goals without a challenge from my subconscious. I decided on the following:

- Does the opportunity/goal **excite** me?
- Does it **challenge** me?
- Does it **strengthen** me?
- Does it **grow** me?
- Does it **motivate** me forward?

I had always wanted to get back to writing, but I'd never really been serious about doing so. I knew I had a book inside me that I wanted to get out, but I had tried a few times to get serious and had always allowed myself to be held back by excuses.

Now, I wasn't willing to allow excuses to be part of my modus operandi any longer. I considered that brush with the bus a clear sign that I was meant to fulfill a purpose. Now I was driven to discover what it was, and I didn't want to end 2016 the same way I started it, no closer to moving forward on any of my long-standing goals.

I didn't have to wait long to try out my speculative theory. That afternoon, a friend posted that she was seeking co-authors for a book she wanted to publish about gratitude. I read the post, ran through my new list of requirements to determine whether I said yes or no, and hopped in with both feet to say **yes**!

I don't know about you, but I view my life differently than some. I believe experiences that flow into my life are divine, including the lessons, the hardships, and the challenges. I've always found that when something is right for me, it will show up and all things will fall into place with ease. Such was the case with this first writing opportunity. It showed up on my Facebook timeline and it just felt right. Saying yes to it opened doors that I never expected, and I found myself experimenting with yes not only for the fifteen days I'd planned to but for the rest of my lifetime!

Through that opportunity, I met many beautiful souls, and several became good friends. One, in particular, invited me on a trip that changed my life's direction in many ways!

As I have moved through life the last three years, I've continued to weigh opportunities, experiences, and decisions by the criteria I decided on that beautiful day in August 2016. So many goals have been achieved, and yet more have been accomplished that I never thought would be. Now, I'd like to share my process with you to help empower you in your life, and if you have not yet lived many of your dreams, now will be a perfect time to begin!

The Power of Yes!

Before I share my practice with you, it might help you to understand how powerful it is by giving you a peek into some of the things I've accomplished since 2016. Much of what I continue to achieve is connected to my willingness to say yes. As I think back and walk through all that I've said yes to over the last three years, it's quite evident that one step led to another and another and another, but it wouldn't have happened if I'd not taken the very first step and decided to go after some things I'd not really worked to pursue, but clearly should have.

- Co-authored a book, *Live in Gratitude Daily*, Aug 2016
- Met a good friend through that opportunity, Dec 2016
- Became comfortable with Facebook lives as a co-author, 2017
- Authored my own book reaching #1 Best Seller and #1 Hottest New Release, Mar 2018
- Said yes to a speaking opportunity in Edmonton, Canada, Sep 2017
- Had a story published in *Chicken Soup for the Soul*, Sept 2017 (Dreams & Premonitions)
- Said yes to a leadership retreat in Costa Rica & speaking opportunity, Oct 2017
- Traveled to US/Canada/Bahamas, Nov 2018
- Became a trackabook publisher, Jan 2019
- Expanded to become a unique VIP hybrid book publisher, June 2019

By weighing opportunities against five simple words, it allows me to say yes quickly or no more efficiently and keeps my subconscious calm. I'm able to assess the benefits of an idea or opportunity more efficiently, and comfortably say yes or no as I determine best.

Let's get you started on moving forward with your goals this year!

Your First Steps

The first step to achieving your most meaningful goals begins with knowing your boundaries for saying yes to things. For example, in my case, when I feel something isn't going to help me grow or it may not strengthen me, or it doesn't excite me, I have no problem saying no to it. After all the years I've lived on this big beautiful earth, I figure I have earned the right and the privilege to say no to a few things and feel good about doing so.

By setting boundaries first, knowing how you will determine whether something is a yes or a no helps you confidently choose your directions in life with much less guilt or doubt. If an opportunity shows up and you feel it isn't a good fit for you at the time, that doesn't mean it may never show up again. If it's meant for you, it will come around again, and maybe next time it will be even better!

The following exercise is unique in its simplicity, yet when it comes to encouraging your subconscious to step back and allow you to experiment with something new that you feel you might want to achieve, this works with amazing ease. Your subconscious steps aside and trusts that you are simply trying something on. Just as you might do when you go to a clothing store: choosing something from a rack, taking it to a changing room, and trying it on. How often have you done that and realized the clothing didn't look as you'd expected?

By choosing five words that will guide you to making every yes and no decision regarding your goals or opportunities, this process allows you to more comfortably try on the opportunity or goal with no judgment or expectation of the outcome. If something doesn't work as you expected it to, you are free to let it go! You are giving yourself permission!

1. List several things an opportunity/goal/experience must do for you (i.e. excite you, stretch you, etc.)
2. List 3-4 goals you've put off and would now like to go after. (Tip: List your longest-standing goals first).
3. Choose your go word. Mine was yes! Yours could be yes or go or kowabunga! Choose something you will enjoy going after time and again!

You have now identified a few goals and how you are going to determine if the opportunities showing up are in alignment with your visions. Now, it's time to watch for opportunities that spring up all around you!

When I began seeking out opportunities, I tried to remain open-minded to everything that showed up. I evaluated the possibilities to determine if they were in alignment with my goals and visions, did they offer me a chance to have fun? Are they going to teach me a new skill or help me to step into a skill as I had secretly wanted to do but hadn't (mine was doing Facebook lives)?

The more fun you can make this exercise, the more readily you will find the doors of opportunity opening to you. It isn't meant to be taken so seriously that you can't have a little fun with it.

When my husband and I were coming home from a trip out West a few years ago, we decided to stop at a place that offered ziplining. We had driven past the sign for years yet had never once decided to stop and explore. This one trip we did, and boy, it was one of the best things we did on the trip home. Now, my husband and I are seeking out ziplining opportunities wherever we travel; we enjoyed our first time so much!

Don't allow the day to pass you by without taking some time to be grateful for what is presenting itself to you. You may never know when an opportunity shows up that changes the trajectory of your life or steers you down a pathway that you never thought was possible.

We all receive 84,500 seconds a day to spend. Some of us choose to spend them making long-lasting memories. Others spend them caring for loved ones or volunteering their time to worthwhile causes. Still, others look for ways to live every moment with an open heart, mind, and spirit!

No matter how you choose to live, may life be filled with all the yeses you wish to achieve. May your yeses lead you to some of the most exciting, fulfilling, rewarding, and beautiful places you have ever wanted to go. May there even be those places you have never thought to include, but now they beckon, welcoming you!

Living day to day and within every moment is incredibly fulfilling. Make every today count for a more rewarding tomorrow and never be afraid to say yes to the amazing possibilities that surround you!

About Judith Richardson Schroeder

Judith began pursuing writing from a very early age and it has been an integral part of who she is since. She is a co-contributor in several collaborative writing opportunities including anthologies, a gratitude journal, and *Chicken Soup for the Soul's Dreams and Premonitions.* She has also authored a book, *One Magnificent Yes!* which hit #1 bestseller and #1 hottest new release less than six hours after its release in March 2018. Judith is currently in the process of updating that title for redistribution to a broader network of retail stores both on and offline.

As a subconscious behaviorist by profession, Judith marvels at the power of our unconscious. Judith loves exploring ways to work with the subconscious. She enjoys sharing her findings through her books, coaching, and most recently by supporting authors as they bring their books to the world!

Judith is a life architect coach and mentor. Most recently she co-founded a uniquely positioned hybrid publishing agency, Carnelian Moon Publishing. She and her business partner help authors of all calibers realize their visions through their writing and help them to discover a broader audience for their work. They offer uniquely positioned opportunities and collaborative experiences designed to support and enhance their author's journeys. Discerning women seeking out a truly unique authoring experience receive a valuable VIP end-to-end concierge-style of services when they work with Judith and her business partner.

When not running their successful companies, Judith and her husband, Kent, enjoy traveling, on the lookout for the next best ziplining adventure or the most beautiful tropical locations to photograph and enjoy. Their next adventure will take them to the beauty of Guatemala. There they will join other heart-centered individuals to help build homes for single mothers and their children. A trip to one of the most significant Mayan ruins in the country will be included.

Judith enjoys family gatherings as often as possible. She loves sharing in the adventures with her five adult children and taking part in life's many blessings, including watching as her granddaughter, Arya, blesses the world with her very own brand of energy and joy.

Judith is currently working on several collaborative trackabooks for future release including the titles *Manifested Blessings, Gifts of Gratitude, Embracing Energy, Soul & Spirit* and more.

Judith is proud to be a bestselling author, an international speaker, a leadership mentor, and part of a unique community of personal development experts. The community gathers and collaborates through a mobile app known as the PDA app. Judith recognizes the importance of giving back and so also offers a mobile app community of her own through her TILA app, also known as *The Inspired Life* app.

Judith is currently pursuing her Ph.D. in philosophy, specializing in transpersonal counseling and acquiring her ministerial designation. Also, a number of writer retreats & training events are planned for the future.

Guidance from Within Coaching

Website (Coaching/Mindscaping): guidancefromwithincoaching.com
Website (Publishing): carnelianmoonpublishing.com
Instagram: youryearofyescoach

Big Bang Me

Angelique Miralles

Little did I know that, as a result of a discussion I had, there would be such a meaningful transformation in my life. Within a few months, there was a new apartment, a new perfectly aligned job offer, and a lovely twin flame partner.

So, I savored the moment as I walked out of a store on a Saturday morning. Just a couple of months later, I smiled big time when the owner kindly advised me to use intention to create the life I wanted.

I had done it, and not only had it worked wonders, but it had also come swiftly. Mind you, this was not the first 180 transformation in my life!

I was feeling grateful, overwhelmed, and living my desired life. My eyes were the ones of a child on Christmas eve, as I could not yet believe it at all. I had left this toxic situation I was stuck in and reshuffled my life at 180°. All this, thanks to a discussion that sparked my setting intentions to receive precious gifts of life, the ones to free myself and expand into my big me.

Freedom is my main value and I will not compromise on it. It may take time for me to decide but I will eventually get there and protect my freedom no matter what.

I was now back in charge of my life, thriving thanks to my own leadership and trusting life. The greatest collaboration had started. Finally, I was aligning my life with my big me!

This is the story I wish to share with you, in all humbleness.

Here are a few of my beliefs:

Everything is possible.
There is always a solution.
Nothing happens by coincidence.

Let me invite you to reflect on your beliefs.

What are your beliefs? A belief is something you hold as truth. What beliefs manifest in your life? When beliefs manifest into our life, it is called a self-fulfilling prophecy. Whatever you believe shapes your life, gives it a direction, and influences what happens. Are you convinced to continue believing what you believe?

Intending is Manifesting

I believe I give my life direction by having intentions. Sometimes I even struggle to believe they can truly happen. What counts is the clarity of my intent and how aligned it is with who I am, with my values and maybe what we call destiny.

Is life written before we are born, like destiny, or are we the ones who influence it? I had been reflecting on this question, had written and played a one-woman self-revelatory theater performance, and still did not have the answer. I was not even sure I would get it someday. Yet, what I discovered along the way was very different.

Some say that it is the journey that counts, not the destination. I come from a family where secrets are like a second skin and I believe this might have contributed to me embarking on learning interpersonal communication. When I started, my communication skills were so poor that I would say the wrong thing, to the wrong person, at the wrong time, and in the wrong way. I would get myself into very embarrassing situations and felt I was in the wrong place, with the wrong people, not embracing my big me.

Life took me on various journeys, and I learned to be tough and strong, to choose and decide but kept a tender heart, a soft emotional side. Only the ones closest to me could see it. Expressing this more widely felt too raw and vulnerable for me to even venture there. So, there I was within my fortress, pretending to be me. People would tell me, in all kind of difficult situations, "You are strong, you will make it." I would cringe inside and wanted to shout and say "No! That is not exactly the way it is." Except I did not because I could not. Some people faced me and my fortress, challenged my sayings and triggered my awareness. You would think that being aware of my challenges meant I could now address them. Unfortunately, that was not the case. I knew and could do nothing about it. Something inside was aching too much, my emotions were too raw, and I felt too vulnerable.

Equally, life kept coming with the perfect packaging, offering special and bespoke experiences to me that reflected my emotional state. In my case, I was gifted with a few parcels of toxic relationships, where I adapted too much to the other person, wanted to please them, and in return got indifference and requests for infinite giving.

I experienced a lot of anger, frustration, and sadness. You name the emotion; I have been there. I gave second, third, and fourth chances to others and gained no more than a sore heart. I started to think I was crazy. I wondered why I was attracting these relationships and most of all, how I could get out of them and far away forever. Actually, saying that I got no more than a sore heart is a pessimistic perspective. During these times, I aimed to understand, read, search, learn, progress, evolve and am now grateful to these people.

Interactions in these relationships helped me to figure out that I wanted to understand what I needed to learn from them, not to repeat the same experiences over. I was done with toxicity. I had lived it fully, studied it in-depth, and wanted something different. Being repeatedly reproached, or hearing I was not good enough, or not as good as others, in addition to interacting with highly unhappy people, was not doing it for me. I had grown within and I knew better. I was strong and determined. This was going to be the end of toxicity and I was going to find the path to sane interactions with authentic and caring people.

What I had not foreseen was that even though the direction was clear, it did not mean that it was going to be easy. It still required me to make major decisions, which impacted other people I truly cared for, to face frustration, to make compromise and more. At some point, I felt I had embarked on a safety boat that could blow at the touch of a needle.

The equilibrium had been broken and it was a tightrope act to travel across the sling to a better world. Toxicity had not only impacted me, but it had done so to those close to me, and at the time, I undervalued this and thrived thinking it was all going to be ok.

What I remembered was that with human beings you can never know what the reaction to a new situation or interaction will be. Nonetheless, I had developed good improvisational skills that helped me think on my feet, yet I was living in a VUCA world: volatile, uncertainty, complex, ambiguous.

As I was getting confident with the progress made, there came a challenging aspect, as if I was being tested that the changes were strong enough. This is when life tested me, and sometimes big time. Except that while I was living the test experience, it was not all necessarily clear. In fact, I tended to feel confused, with blurred vision, or just aware that I was not reaching my full potential.

And life keeps on testing you, proposing challenging experiences: the ones that make you grow, mostly once you care to analyze and reflect on them, which take time and effort. In the worst cases, you may interact within toxic relationships at work or at home, facing a challenging time, wondering why this all happens to you. Maybe events are just unfolding and not happening to anyone in particular. Nonetheless, we may feel that it is happening to us.

So, here we are, in the middle of a storm, or even a hurricane, and feeling overwhelmed with what is going on. It might be difficult to keep a clear head, to think, to pause. Emotions are taking over or, on the contrary, dullness is ruling, and we are feeling empty of energy, let alone motivation. You feel incomplete; you get a sense you have lost your light. You know you are bigger than what you currently express in this precise moment, that you can reach higher, that you still have winning poker cards in your pocket. Except the cards are stuck as if they had been solidly glued together on both sides and you cannot separate them anymore. And if you try to pull the cards out, you will tear some pieces and not get the full card. The fact is, human beings are so varied that we all react in a different way to what we live.

Taking Small Steps

In order to come out and reach a better weather forecast in our life, decisions and actions need to be taken. Nothing is going to happen unless you give it a direction. And to give it a direction, you need to release yourself from the situation and its emotions and gather back your big me together. So, waiting is totally unproductive and leads nowhere. Taking small steps unlocks situations. You hold your life in your hand and the more aligned with who you genuinely are, the more events will unfold in total flow. Yes, you may be really surprised!

Calling in the Big Me

Lift your head and come out of the dark clouds. Have a discussion, take a long walk, play with your pet, or whatever works for you. It is all about taking the first step into clearing your mind, body, and emotional field to move towards finding a solution. The solution lies inside you, in your big me person.

Now you may wonder what I call big me. Well big me is you: your full potential expressed. It comes gradually, step by step; in fact, it is by aligning and setting intentions that you call in the big me back into you. I say back into you because it has most likely been scattered around, like pieces of soul, in the different relationships and places you have been.

And when we are stuck in one relationship, it is not because of the people involved, it is because our big me wants to get their pieces back but cannot yet access them. As long as you have not felt the magic of the big me reconstruction, you will feel incomplete or uncomfortable.

I believe that all that you have been living so far in your life has a purpose. Looking at the big picture of your life, on your own or with the support of a third neutral person, will lead you into understanding more of yourself and your potential.

In my case, I was fully aware that I did not wish to stay in the situations I was in. I started reflecting but there was always something in the way of truly acting. Hearing comments from people around me helped me realize that I could no longer stay where I was, and that action needed to be taken. Except I had to find the direction, the how, and the determination to put all of that into practice.

At some point, I had a long exchange with one of my sons. I asked him what he would do if he were me. It surely was an uncomfortable question for him, and I explained that I needed to hear outsider views of my situation to understand how it came across. This is the way I function when I am in doubt about something. I have plenty of discussions with different people and gradually gauge their responses against my own values—things that are important to me and out of which I make decisions—and my wishes before deciding, prioritizing and finally acting. If you are more of an introvert, you may get there in a different way, maybe by reflecting while walking on your own. How you get to clarity is not important, yet the clarity you get is key to moving forward. And here we are talking about expanding into your big me and your desired world. Imagine what it might be like!

Sensing the Guides

In any case, it is our inner feelings that guide us into what is good for us or not. It really all happens inside. This means the more you are connected to your inner self, the more you are likely to hear, feel, and sense your inner signals. Acting upon these inner signals is what I call inner leadership, the one that is authentic because it starts from inside and makes it way out naturally.

It took me years to listen to myself. I had been guided and conditioned rather deeply and every time my authentic me was swiftly popping up, it was quieted by thoughts of, "You cannot do this, your father paid for your studies." or "You will do like such and such, study German, move to England." Except I wanted to be an artist, study English, and move to the US. I was clearly being redirected from my own path, and surely so with the best intentions ever. This, I never doubted.

I managed it all, in its own time, with a bit a determination and alignment. Yes, it all happened, unfolded, unrolled, and manifested. I believed in it so much, that I am convinced it has influenced the outcome of my success. Many times, I marvel at the magic of life. And I feel grateful for life, the universe, and my soul.

Inner Leadership

I am a lifelong learner and I love to analyze what I could have done better in order to reach even more success. My takeaway is the ability to influence, create, and make things happen authentically and aligned with who I am. Finally, my big me had some space to exist and optimistically address my desired world: The world is my oyster.

The world is your oyster means that you can achieve anything you wish in life or go anywhere because you have the opportunity or ability to do so. (ref: https://www.bellenglish.com/news/world-your-oyster-phrase-week)

Bell English explains that a desired state is the result of having the opportunity or ability to achieve anything you wish for in life. One could also call it the destination. As you know, many claim that when traveling, the most important thing is the journey as opposed to the destination itself. This chapter speaks about journeying from an unsatisfactory state into a desired one, creating a state of inner brilliance, and this is what I call inner leadership. It all happens inside and becomes visible in the world once ready. The path to reaching the desired world has the following stages: *stop, set, go.* I will describe in step later in the chapter.

Living in Alignment

Coming back to the discussion I had with my son, I would say the outcome, after self-reflection, was to set objectives. One of them was to significantly increase my income. Within three months it started to happen. Six months later, I was feeling totally overwhelmed, in deep gratitude and still struggling to realize it had all happened magically! I experienced full manifestation of my intentions. I had some new projects and clients coming in, using the same skillset in different contexts, as well as some interesting job offers coming my way. On my side, what I had done was to update my curriculum vitae and the social media I am present on. Barely three months after setting intentions, I started having some companies contact me for interviews. My aim was to let it come and go with what felt right, innately knowing that if I chose to, the jobs were for me. This allowed me to be fully authentic, speak my truth during lengthy interviews, and obtain great offers. In the process, I felt so self-assured, so blunt, that I played with it and laughed. I was offered a position. I had to make a choice: full-time employment after 23 years as a freelancer or keeping up with being an external, independent provider. My interviewers called me a free spirit and I felt wonderfully proud of having come across as who I am. My inner leadership advised me to favor the experience of full-time employment and I followed along. The only permanent thing in life is impermanence.

Time passes, work has had its challenges and lessons, but I feel an overall alignment with who I am and my skillset. **I sense that I am at the right place, having the highest impact I may have, and this is very important to get a feeling of completeness and self-realization.** My purpose in that position is **to contribute to raising people's awareness** and leadership.

The magic is when during leadership programs, attendees start speaking about the soul, the divine, the feminine, the masculine, and other deep topics. I always feel my full presence and smile when it comes up, to honor what has emerged. In these moments I feel realized as a human being and find meaning to life. They are so deep and connected, I am touched and honored to be who I am. Most of my clients go through life-changing transitions, sometimes painfully and my job is to connect them back to who they are and equip them with the finest skills to do so. They are developing into shining their big me.

Not long ago, one of my clients was questioning herself deeply on her poor sense of self-realization, and how it had created a painful value conflict within her. She was struggling to fully embody her big me as she realized she was not in the right place and not doing the right job for her soul. That got me into a very deep place of self-contemplation. Who am I? Where is this transformational power coming from?

Who am I?

I ask myself these questions because I am aware that I am in control of nothing else than ensuring I am aligned and authentic. For the rest, I feel comfortable diving deep as far as the soul root, meeting emotions and acknowledging them fully.

Often, my overall feeling in full presence, is to honor the man or woman I have in front of me and who I am working with. In these moments, I feel like a soul awakener, the sparkle that lights it up, the one that does not even need wind or oxygen to create a flame.

And the more I deepen my relationship with myself and my own experience, the more magical it gets for me and for others. I have learned to accept what comes my way, to feel uncomfortable, and most of all, to shine with no limits when necessary. This is what I am inviting you to do. I am inviting you to join me on this journey. Because you are reading this book, I understand that you may be part of my tribe and I feel very strongly about my tribe, the ones that are looking to shine their big me.

My Even Bigger Me

In the meantime, I am still struggling with being overweight—gained during the toxic interactions—and my new ailment I developed during the toxic interactions: hypertension. I also experience moments of anxiety, vulnerability, and rawness despite the big me being out. This has made me realize that there might be different levels of soul awakening.

Hence, I am embarking on a new development path for the big me to come into full expression. Reading a post on social media, I saw the beaming profile picture of a person and thought, "What do I need to fully shine my big me?"

It gradually set into me and I spontaneously asked a therapist if he could help. He uncovered my feelings of being trapped in a cage. I booked an appointment and let it go so much that I nearly fell asleep on his table. The next few days were a challenge as the stress was leaving my body and I was feeling so tranquil and sleepy that I could hardly believe it.

I knew I had touched on something meaningful. The big me needs space, as well as body, emotional, and soul updates in order to flourish, it just doesn't happen at the snap of a finger, it is a true ever-evolving journey. I even got thinking that it might be life's purpose to fully express one's own big me.

Energy is the Secret

Let me tell you how all this energetic big me stuff started. It was soon after breaking up a relationship and while struggling to let go, that a friend of mine told me about recuperating my pieces of big me from the relationship. Hearing this triggered the need to call another friend, who confirmed this. I was hoping she would do it for me, but she said I could do it and explained to me how to do it.

It was the third time in my life that I was given the keys to unlock on a soul level. Each time has been very similar. There I was, hoping to get some external help, while being fully aware of my power, and hearing that I was the one to do it and that I had what it took. Needless to say, imagine how uncomfortable and scary this was. I was being required to step into my big me even further.

In my bed one evening, I started out and cleaned all the pieces of light, energy, and big me that I had left in the relationship and in the places we had been living and existing together. The morning after, like magic, I felt no more attachment. It felt weird and new. Transactional games did not have any impact on my heart anymore and I felt relieved. Conducting such an energy session for myself had tremendously helped me and allowed me to start afresh.

Since then, I have heard many stories of people struggling with similar issues and who are struggling to retrieve their light, their big me pieces. This is why I am now helping others do just this.

The other thing I have learned is to let go and help others get rid of the emotional baggage we store in the deep tissues of our bodies. It is called emotional detox. One shocking anecdote is that during a workshop, as I was emotionally detoxifying my partner, he seemed to momentarily have left his body and I really thought he was dead, that I had killed him, with my big me. I went into a great panic until he gradually came back to himself, thanks to the help of the trainer. I did not know what I was feeling anymore, it was totally overwhelming. Especially as on my side, I had also experienced the most powerful bodily experience and was completely taken over by energy, like I was deeply cleaned and finally came out anew. These powerful energetic approaches, especially when combined together, can do wonders to support the coming out of the big me in each and every one of us. I invite you to step in!

Step Into Your Big Me

This work is an invitation to each one of you to step into your big me, be authentic and a leader of your life, become free of your societal conditioning, explore your true nature and fully express who you truly are. This is a simple process I use with clients worldwide to help them step into their big me.

- **Stop: Pausing and breathing**

  Stopping means allowing presence, hence awareness to be. Today's rhythms in society stop this from happening. So, you have to decide to stop. Maybe altogether or go for a conscious walk. Stopping means connecting and paying attention to all your senses because that is where the answers lie. By senses I mean, what you feel, hear, see, smell, taste, and what your intuition tells you. You will feel this in your body, not in your mind. This will subsequently allow you to get moving, establish priorities, make decisions, and go into the given direction. Feelings never lie.

STEP INTO YOUR *BIG ME*

•Set: Adopting a different perspective

Once you are in that state, call upon your imagination. From these feelings, what image comes to mind, what sense is triggered, what does it remind you of? Looking forward, invite yourself to imagine big time. Change perspective a few times. Then ask yourself:

o What am I learning from this experience?
o What opportunity does this experience give me?
o How will I come out of it once it is over?

•Go: Setting the direction

It is now time to decide on the direction you wish to give your life. Visualize it, feel it, just like it has already happened. Set intentions. Make sure you have gathered all your pieces of big me.

- o Where do I wish to get to?
- o What does it feel like?
- o What are my intentions?
- o Where have I left pieces of my big me? In places? Relationships?

It is time to give another direction to your life, to decide, and act. Are you ready?

About Angelique Miralles

Developing, Coaching, Authoring, Inspiring

Born in: Saint Peter's Clinic, on Angels 'Street

Her DNA says she is 100% European, with a slight tip for Southern Europe at 53.7% (Iberian 30.7%, Sardinian 12.0%, and Italian 10.9%), and the rest belonging to Northern and Western Europe with a smaller 46.4% (Scandinavian 21.7%; West & North European 14.8%; Brittany, Irish, Scottish & Welsh 9.9%)

And that makes 100% of Me.

I am peculiar, so here is a summary of some peculiar facts of my life:

- I've lived in six different countries.
- I have three children in three different countries birthed in three different ways—traditional, Dutch, & water + lotus birth—I love experimenting!
- I've had three meaningful relationships.
- I've learned seven languages and I've forgotten three.
- I'm a well-traveled global citizen.
- I love human beings and diversity with all my heart.

While I consider myself a woman of purpose, a multifaceted spontaneous artist, and a soul awakener, sense is what motivates me. I need to understand. My mindset is one of curiosity. And I can equally choose to be with myself only, at ease with silence and my own company.

Others say that I possess a unique quality of wisdom and sharp insight in assisting men and women to reconnect with their essential nature and their inner leadership, so they can access their authentic expression in life.

I have a few key processes I use to enable people to access and express their innate leadership. My aim is to assist clients in cultivating depth, vibrancy, and intimacy in their daily lives, professional lives, and relationships.

Over the last 21 years, my deep-level work has facilitated powerful transformations in the lives of the many I have worked with. A certified executive coach and leadership facilitator, I have worked for top multinationals across industries and organizational levels. An emotional detox practitioner together with a soul retriever ability allows me to go deeper into what is needed for the expression of self, of the big me. You can find more information on my dedicated site: www.e-motiondeep.com

I have a lifetime of dedication to understanding human beings across cultures and on all levels. Through my own inner process and by assisting many globally, I have the capacity to efficiently and effectively cut through to the deepest issues and provide proven solutions to navigate through one's inner world and make it flourish. It may take time, but we will get there.

My purpose is to contribute to raising people's awareness and help them develop interpersonal skills, a global collaborative mindset, and self-leadership. I work alongside people like you who are aiming to achieve the best in their life and act authentically.

This work is an invitation to each one of you to step into your big me, be authentic and a leader of your life, by becoming free of your societal conditioning, explore your true nature, and fully express who you truly are.

Are you ready to step in?

Coaching with Angelique

Website: www.coaching-leadership.net

Website: www.e-motiondeep.com

Now What

Janet Wiszowaty

"To be yourself in a world that is constantly trying to make you something else is the greatest accomplishment."

—Ralph Waldo Emerson

Beginning

Once upon a time . . . wait, this is not a fairy tale, this is about a young woman who lived the first part of her life wearing a mask of confidence. Very few people saw that she was not really the self-confident person she betrayed. Even her mother, when she found her crying after a breakup with a boyfriend, told her that she was the most confident person she knew. I did not set out to be a police officer's wife, in fact my goal was to marry my high school boyfriend and become the wife of a farmer in a small Manitoba town. That was until the day he told me he was taking a "friend" from out of town to the wedding we had been invited to as a couple. I left that small town and moved to the big city of Winnipeg. Little did I know that this 18-year-old's life was about to take a total shift.

My grandfather helped me get my first job in the city and it was there while on a lunch break that I bumped into a friend of my father's. Henry took pity on this young woman in the big city by herself and invited me out for dinner. I had a night class that night but who in their right mind was going to turn down a free dinner? As it turned out, he took me to my future mother-in-law's house where they were having a going-away party for her niece. Her son, Les, opened the door in answer to Henry's knock and as we walked in, Henry handed Les the keys to his vehicle and told Les he was going to be driving this strange young girl home that night. That was December 6, 1971. We were married the following July 1972.

Life was a bit of a whirlwind and now I was a wife; then before our first anniversary I was the wife of a police officer, then two months after my 20th birthday, I became a mom and a year later I became the mother of two children. Who was I? I just moved along trying to keep up, yet in hindsight, I was living my life for everyone else and had no idea that there was so much more out there. I had a part-time job that helped with the bills and looked after my family. There were many nights I cried myself to sleep worrying about the money and if I was a good mom while leaving my children to go to work. I was planning daycare around my husbands shift work, selling our home, and moving to another province by myself with two babies while my husband had already gone to his new post from Manitoba to British Columbia. Years later, while working as an insurance clerk we would ask women what they did . . . they would answer they were a housewife. I would suggest they put down domestic engineer.

My Aha Moment

Our mindset can keep us stuck. At the time, the title housewife had no value to me. Soon after, I quit my job because I did not have a babysitter that I was comfortable with—this was the second time I had done this. The first time was when we lived on the Queen Charlotte Islands (now known as Haida Gwaii), and once again, I was crying at night because I was worried about what I was doing to my children by sending them to a babysitter as they would go crying. It was affecting my health, at 27 I had developed stomach ulcers. So, as I'd done before, I quit my job and looked after other people's children while looking after my own. Don't get me wrong, there are great caregivers out there, it just was not what I would have chosen because I liked going to work and being with other people. I didn't know at the time it was tied in with my self-esteem.

During that time, I decided to stay home with my two young children while my husband went on the road for a year. He managed to make it home about three weeks out of that year but basically, I was on my own. We had no family nearby as they were three provinces away. My world was my kids, my home, and socializing/gossiping with other mothers. Yes, gossiping. It was years later, after I had trained with Jack Canfield, that I would see that this was a mirror of my life. A life that I had not put any value on, so I talked about other people's lives.

When Les came home to stay, he realized I hadn't spent any money on myself and asked me why. I had not bought anything for myself because I did not feel worthy of getting anything. I was not working; I did not consider babysitting and being paid for it as a job. My self-worth was tied up in a paycheck. Yes, that was my realization. If I did not receive a paycheck, I did not feel I had the right to spend money on myself. It had nothing to do with the fact that my husband had a paycheck and I had full access and paid the bills, and he never once made any comments on how I spent it. What an aha moment that was.

It was shortly after that realization that a job opportunity came my way that I never would have thought or dreamed of. It was not in my realm of consciousness to even consider applying for such a job. Again, mindset fits in here, until we are pulled out of our comfort zone, we do not see anything outside of that box. Jack Canfield's events are always held at five-star hotels, why? The same reason you buy a new car when you are just looking. Once you experience sitting in a brand-new car, you want one. Once you stay in a five-star hotel, you never want to stay in a Motel 6 again. By the way, there is nothing wrong with staying in a Motel 6, it is usually attached to a budget. When you experience the higher quality, your brain starts working on how you can afford to do this again.

In the fall of 1981, I started a temporary position in the administrative communications center of the Royal Canadian Mounted Police (RCMP). It was here that I began to grow and realize my worth. It was the beginning of the journey to who I am today and who I am today is light years away from who I was then, and it was because of a woman I was blessed to work with. There is a saying that you are the five people you surround yourself with. Liz came into my life and forever changed it. She was also a police officer's wife and even though she had a master's degree in education, she was working in this position. Like many RCMP wives, we have to adapt and reinvent ourselves when our spouses get transferred and thus was the case with Liz. There were no teaching jobs available in Victoria when they were transferred there.

"Because one believes in oneself, one doesn't try to convince others. Because one is content with oneself, one doesn't need others' approval. Because one accepts oneself, the whole world accepts him or her."

—Lao-Tzu

Discovering My Self-Worth

Who would have thought this girl from a little Manitoba town, who had not finished high school and was told she wasn't smart enough to go to university so there was no need to spend another year in school to pick up the two courses she needed graduate, would ever be recommended for higher education? Not me. Remember that thing called mindset? Well, my mind was set, and it was not in my realm of consciousness that I could further my education. So, I was surprised and somewhat astonished that my new friend, Liz, would actually mention me going back to school. She finally convinced me to take a college entrance exam and apply to attend. To my surprise, I passed and was accepted into Camosun College in Victoria, plus I was informed I was writing at a first-year university level. This coming from a person who had never taken grade 12 English. Then, we got transferred.

Even though I was leaving a job that I really liked, I now had an opportunity to turn it into a career. We went off to the only city I told Les I would never live in: Vancouver, British Columbia. I learned in my training with Jack Canfield, and other teachers and mentors, that energy flows where attention goes, and my attention was focused on not going to Vancouver. We spent eight years in the Lower Mainland of British

Columbia, and I have to honestly say that what I had dreaded the most turned into my biggest growth. I had a career, we lived in a beautiful home, and our children were happy and healthy. I learned so much about myself during that time and even had the courage to quit my job when my health was compromised due to stress.

I want to expand on this a little. The stress was not due to my job, I loved my job. The stress was due to politics and management. I believe that is why most people become ill—when they do not stay true to themselves nor are comfortable enough to leave a toxic environment. Then there is the expectation of others. When I told my parents I had quit my job they both separately said, "What are you going to do? How are you going to pay your bills?" I always tried to live up to my father's expectations of me and I always felt I could not live up to those expectations. Again, when I took the various personal development courses, I learned that no one can make you feel inferior if you do not let them. We teach people how to treat us, and in this case, although I went back to the emotions of my childhood, I did not let them know how much what they had said hurt me. Les and I both had the confidence in our decision, and to be judged as if we were being irresponsible was disheartening.

When we first moved to Vancouver, I did not have the courage to apply to another college or university, but I did not abandon my new knowledge that I was smart enough to continue my education. I learned there was a Knowledge Network on TV where I could take a course in private; confidence doesn't always extend to the risk of being judged. I signed up for an Introductory Psychology course and was diligent in watching my weekly program after Les had faithfully taped the sessions on the VCR when I was working. I would then watch the class on my days off. I managed to pass the correspondence course with a B, so I signed up for another psychology course on behavior and passed that one too. After the first course, the professor contacted me and asked if I would come on the program so that he could interview me. His intention was to show his audience that they too could advance their education. If a mother of two with a full-time job as a shift worker could do it, so could they.

I continued to grow and take more risks. When I quit my job of six years because of my health, I chose to go to university full-time. I got up the courage to apply to Simon Fraser University in Burnaby, British Columbia. When what you are doing is no longer working for you, try something else. I got accepted and preferred to go to classes during the day and to support my education and keep the bills paid, I chose to work as a relief police dispatcher in my previous communications center as well as for two other police detachments. I know you are probably thinking, why is she going back to the place she said was so toxic? Well, when we shift our mindset, other things shift with it. You see, I was now totally in control of my life. I chose to go to school and pick courses I liked, and I chose the days and times I would work. The more you have the courage to take the reins of your time and do what you love, the more self-confidence you have and the more your self-esteem grows.

E + R = O

I was two years into my new routine of running my now teenage children to their bowling and riding lessons plus high school activities, attending classes during the day, and working several night shifts a week when my husband applied for a promotion. This was a great career move for him and he did get the promotion. The new position just happened to be in Toronto, Ontario, three provinces away. Remember, branches move with the wind and break only when the wind gets too severe. We can create the turbulence with our thoughts and actions. I supported Les in this career move even though I would have to basically start over again. I now had to look for another job, apply to another university, and take the kids away from their friends and social activities. By then, Tamara was becoming quite the equestrian and Kristopher was in grade 11. There will always be changes in your life, maybe not to the same degree that happened in our lives, but changes will occur, nonetheless. In chapter one of Jack Canfield's book, *The Success Principles*, titled *Take 100% Responsibility For Your Life*, he shares a formula that shifted my mindset again. This formula is E + R = O. You are probably wondering now what in the heck is that?

It can be life-changing when you work the formula. I was able to see how I had been wiser than I thought I was in the past. When we lived in Sooke, I received a call from one of the spouses telling me she had heard Les was having an affair. Well, he was a pretty good-looking police officer and there had been a letter from a woman saying she wanted to have an affair with him. He showed me the letter then wrote her one back but that is a whole other story. Anyhow, I did not put much regard in the rumor, then I received a call from another spouse saying the same thing, so I decided to take some action. I found a babysitter, went and got my hair done, got dressed up, and showed up at Les's office to surprise him for lunch. We ate in the cafeteria with his colleagues and when they left to go back to their office, I asked him if he was having an affair. He looked at me and did not say a word. I have to say, if he had been having an affair, he deserved a medal because he was at work every day, taught a motorcycle class most weekends, and was home every night. Here is the formula:

Event (E) + Reaction (R) = Outcome (O)

- **Event**: The rumor that Les was having an affair.
- **Reaction**: I asked him.
- **Result**: We are still married today.

This could have had a totally different outcome if I had taken it as the truth and packed up my kids and left without asking him or waited until we had a disagreement and throw it up in his face. Both could have resulted in a divorce. How we do anything is how we do everything. We always, always have a choice. Even though my self-esteem at the time was low, the value of my marriage and the love for my husband gave me the courage and strength to step out of my comfort zone and get down to the truth of the matter. I had a life plan, one made from inside a box of limited knowledge, thus a mindset that would have kept me from having the life I enjoy today. We are all on a journey and sometimes it is best we do not know where it will lead. From the girl who thought she would marry a farmer and live happily ever after on the farm to a girl who has traveled all across Canada and has had the privilege of living and working in four provinces and one territory. I have traveled the world, studied in Greece and in Italy taking travel university courses. Now I do not set limitations on what I do and where I go. I changed my mantra from "I can't afford it." to "How can I afford it?" That has allowed me to travel and train with some of the best teachers and spend time with some of the best mentors. I travel to retreats that feed my soul and connect me with more wonderful people and stretches me until I think I can stretch no more. Someone said to me a while ago, "You have a great life." and I answered her with "I created it."

In 2010, while on a seven-day workshop titled, *Breakthrough to Success*, there was a worksheet we were tasked with filling out. It was called *My Success Form*. The instructions on the worksheet told us to divide our life into three equal age periods then write three successes we had in the first third of our life. In my first third, I put down that my successes were: 1) getting my horse, Princess—I was 14 and having a horse had been a dream ever since I can remember; 2) becoming Carnival Queen—when I was 16, I became our small town's Carnival Queen; 3) meeting and marrying Les. In my second third, I put down that my successes were: 1) working for the RCMP and becoming a civilian member of the RCMP; 2) getting accepted into and going to university; 3) going to and becoming involved with Marriage Encounter—a retreat for couples with good marriages designed to help enhance them by giving couples tools for success. In my last third, I put down that my successes were: 1) traveling to Rome and Greece on university courses—I earned six credits while going overseas and studying for three weeks; 2) getting certified to do FISH! workshops in Canada—FISH! is based on the philosophy of the Seattle Pike Place Fish Market: "Be There, Play, Make Their Day, and Choose Your Attitude"; 3) taking Jack Canfield's workshops—I am now a Canfield certified trainer in The Success Principles™ and The Success Principles™ methodology.

There was a place to put what I wanted to accomplish in the next five years, and I accomplished two of them in a modified way. My goals were to: 1) to become a successful keynote speaker—I spoke in the United Nations in New York in June 2017. It wasn't a keynote nor was it within the five years. I do not consider it a failure, but rather that I manifested something amazing after the five years. 2) to cruise the Nile for my 60th birthday and while I can't remember what I did for my 60th, I have cruised to Alaska and the Caribbean. 3) I did not become a bestseller of two books within those five years, however, I have been a contributing author in three books since 2010. What some people might see as failure I see as accomplishments and successes in motion and I allow my goals and visions to present themselves in ways that low self-esteem and a limited mindset would never have allowed.

"Never be bullied into silence. Never allow yourself to be made a victim. Accept no one's definition of your life; define yourself."

—Harvey Fierstein

My Success Form

This information was taken from The Canfield Training Group © 2010

My Success Form Directions: Divide your life into three equal age periods (i.e. birth–15, 16–30, 31–45) and list three successes for each period on the spaces provided below. In the last section, list three successes you would like to have in the next five years.

FIRST THIRD:

1.

2.

3.

SECOND THIRD:

1.

2.

3.

THIRD THIRD:

1.

2.

3.

NEXT 5 YEARS:

1.

2.

3.

Janet Wiszowaty of Worldly Connektions is a Jack Canfield Success Principals Certified Trainer www.familyconnekt.com

About Janet Wiszowaty

Janet Wiszowaty was married at 18, became the mother of two children by age 22, and has had to recreate herself many times over. Within a year of her marriage, her husband joined Canada's elite police force, the Royal Canadian Mounted Police (RCMP) and the life she thought she was about to have changed to one of a series of transitions and adventures. Janet was used to moving from place to place with her parents, now it was with her husband to four provinces, nine cities/towns and 15 homes before settling in Edmonton—not her forever home, she has itchy feet. Eventually, she joined the RCMP as an emergency police dispatcher and a whole new series of challenges was introduced.

As a police dispatcher, she saw a new world of challenges that people were experiencing and after a diagnosis of post-traumatic stress disorder (PTSD) in 2003, a new journey began. She sought professional help that took her on the road to recovery and then one day was told she didn't need to see the psychologist anymore. Her response was, "**Now What?**" Thus, the journey she is presently on is to support women on their **now what** personal journeys with one-on-one coaching, her workshops, and referrals to her network of inspiring people.

When Janet reached her now what moment, she decided to go back to university, became certified to do FISH! workshops in Canada, trained with Jack Canfield and became certified in The Success Principles™, trained with Marcia Wieder and became certified as a Dream Coach®, then studied Neuro-Linguistic Programing (NLP), Time Line Therapy®, and hypnotherapy. With every bump in the road, turbulent times serve us all, even if we do not realize it at the time. Janet brings all of her experience, including her 30 years of experience as an emergency police dispatcher and all the learning she has done through her now what moments to serve and assist you during those bumpy and turbulent times.

Chief Connektor of Worldly Connektions

Host of Worldly Connektions podcast

Co-author in *The Power to Change* & *No B.S. Truth: What It Really Takes to Build A Successful Business*

Certified Canfield Success Principles™ Trainer

MNLP, MTLT, MCHt, MNLPC

International Speaker & Workshop Conductor

Worldly Connektions
Website: www.familyconnekt.com
Facebook: www.facebook.com/YourNowWhatCoach
LinkedIn: http://linkedin.com/in/challengesdealtwith

The Positive Side of a Crushing Experience

Deborah Ann Davis

"It's going to be alright," said a soft voice floating from somewhere above me. It was meant to feel soothing, but if the truth be told, it was exceedingly irritating. The voice continued, "Just remain calm, and—"

"Why are you talking like that?" I snapped as irritation won out over good manners. "I don't mean to be rude, but could you stop?" I was one seriously cranky 19-year-old kid.

Looking back, I find it so odd I didn't notice that I couldn't really see anything. I didn't wonder where the voice was coming from, or where I was. I wasn't curious as to why it was raining inside a car on a sunny day or that instead of it being mid-afternoon, suddenly it was nighttime. I didn't even wonder why I was on the floor of my boyfriend's vehicle.

All I knew, in my shock-induced little bubble, was that I was kneeling under the dashboard with my shoulders arched over the edge of the passenger seat and that my back was bothering me almost as much as that stupid voice. Every time I tried to haul myself back onto the seat that infuriating speech would start up again.

Isn't shock one of the greatest tricks produced by the human body? It kept me from understanding that our car had been slammed on my side by a drunk driver. It conveniently provided tunnel vision to prevent me from seeing my two broken legs, or the fact that my boyfriend was dripping blood on me as he struggled to keep me awake. It turned a horrific situation into a dreamlike state where I didn't feel panic. But, most importantly, shock kept me from feeling any pain. Although the accident occurred in 1977, long before cell phones were invented, the positive ripples from that event affect me even today. And, yes, I said *positive* ripples.

Luck Was on My Side

I'm pretty sure the drunk driver hit our vehicle around 3:00 p.m. on a sunny Sunday afternoon, interrupting our leisurely drive back to the University of Massachusetts campus after a family visit in Boston. Ours was the only car on that country back road, and because the other driver was so drunk, his car was barreling along in the grass on the wrong side of the road. Even though we were the only two vehicles out there, he managed to drive up on the pavement just in time to crush my side of the car.

I still don't remember that at all. Lucky, right? Plus, the accident couldn't have happened in a better place. There were no other vehicles around to collide with our crash. We were driving backroad speeds, not highway speeds, which would've made the impact far greater. My boyfriend and I were the only injured people so when help finally came, we had their full attention. Luck was definitely on our side.

How about the fact that the next car that came along just happened to have a first responder in it, an EMT? She sent her car ahead to get help while she climbed into the back seat of our car to aid us. I don't remember her at all, except for her annoyingly calm voice. Apparently, I was lucid enough to give her my parents' contact info—although I don't remember doing that either. I was later told that the drunk received a cut on his head, which didn't require stitches, and he skipped out before he could be charged with drunk driving. Luckily, he was driving a company car, so their insurance covered our medical bills.

How Did We Ever Function Without Cellphones?

While the EMT took care of us the best she could, the rest of her party sped off to find a phone they could borrow. Once the ambulance arrived, they took over. Hours later, the EMT called my parents to see how I had fared. Although it was about 9:00 p.m., no one had yet notified them. "Lady," growled my dad at the EMT, "get off my phone!"

If you're a millennial, that may sound harsh. But if you're old enough to remember the '70s, you know there was no call waiting or caller ID back then. Anytime the house phone was in use, no one else could get through. The EMT had to get off the phone before the hospital could contact my family. My dad made one quick call to get my younger sister back home and then waited with my mom for the hospital's call, which didn't come until a couple of hours later.

Meanwhile, my sister and her boyfriend were out on a date somewhere. Using CB radios, the cutting-edge tech of the day, his parents were able to locate the two of them through friends and get her home. By the time the hospital called, all of my family was present for the news that I was going to make it, of course.

Doctor, There's Something Wrong

I don't know what they gave me at the hospital, but after the shock wore off, I still had no pain. Granted, I was a little loopy when I arrived. I kept cracking jokes to cheer up the extremely grim ambulance guys, none of which I remember, but it earned me visits from them until I left the hospital, and yes, I was most definitely medicated while I was in intensive care. However, everyone continuously ignored my attempts to tell them something was wrong. Could it have been because I kept forgetting I had been in an accident? Or, perhaps because I would fall asleep mid-sentence? Who knows?

The only definite thing was that they disregarded my efforts to get them to look at my foot. I guess they assumed that since I had two broken legs, I was confused about that particular complaint. But eventually, someone humored me and pulled back the blanket to look at my foot. The next thing I knew, I was being prepped for surgery. One of my feet had swollen to the point where the cast was cutting into it, so the whole thing had to be reset. I'll never know how I maintained my focus on my foot while in this drugged, half-awake, mostly asleep state, especially when I felt no pain, but thank goodness that nurse took a peek. I also realized, in some fuzzy way, there was something wrong with my hand, which no one but me cared about.

"Doctor, it hurts when I do this."

"Then, don't do that."

A classic joke, but it didn't help the thumb that happened to be broken—diagnosed by the second hospital I attended. The third mistake I can't really blame them for. I arrived at the hospital covered in blood from a gash on my forehead, with more dripping from somewhere on my scalp. Searching for the source of the blood, they shaved back my hair. It was not a good look. Turns out it wasn't my blood after all. If only they had looked a little southwardly, they may have noticed that I had re-broken my nose, but that also went undetected for quite a while.

Make no mistake about it, I'm eternally grateful for the care I received, oversights and all. I happily exist today because of those wonderful underpaid, overworked caregivers. I share the mistakes here because they later contributed to the lowest point of my young life, followed by—spoiler alert—the most powerful life-changing understanding. More on that later.

Recuperation is the history of reaching hundreds of tiny milestones. Graduating high school was so exciting, what with my whole life waiting for me to jump in, but it pales in comparison to having the intravenous drip replaced by solid food. The thrill of my first ballet solo was nothing compared to being able to ditch the catheter and function on my own. I was rocking that recovery! It's the little things that count.

How to Handle an Emergency

Soon after I left the intensive care unit, I grew strong enough to use that little triangular trapeze-thingy dangling overhead to help myself sit up on my own. Talk about exciting and exhausting! Once I harnessed my bodily functions, it was time to relocate. On that momentous day, they packed me into an ambulance and drove me to the UMass Infirmary, where I would spend the rest of the semester. That was one of the strangest days of my life.

Typically, the infirmary experienced a trickle of walk-ins and athletic injuries, but I arrived in the midst of a full-blown emergency—a school bus collision. The parking lot was filled with ambulances unloading injured children. People were rushing around, taking vitals, bandaging, triaging, searching for loved ones. It was a madhouse.

My EMTs moved me and my wheelchair into the waiting room and went to see how they could help. Horrified, I tried not to stare at the victims lining the walls. You know that feeling where you can't help but look, and you know you shouldn't because you're afraid of what you'll see? It was awful . . . until I realized most of them were giggling. Well, if they could be cheerful, so could I. Calming myself down, I was determined to wait until every last one of them had been cared for.

"Ah-choo!" I was helplessly staring at the middle-schooler across from me when he sneezed. To my horror, the force of his sneeze slid the bloody bandage covering one damaged eye off his head and plopped it into his lap. "Oops!" He scooped it up and replaced it backward. "My bad." Raising it up, he turned the blood-soaked gauze around, but it collapsed in his fingers. Annoyed, he peered at it.

"Hey, 'scuse me, how's this supposed to go?" he asked a nurse hurrying by.

"Don't worry about it," she said kindly with a wink.

"Could you take it? It's getting on my pants."

"Sure." She balled up the mess and tossed it into a nearby garbage can and scurried away. The boy rubbed his eyes and nudged the wheelchair-bound kid next to him.

"What's wrong with you?"

"I think my leg is supposed to be broken, or cut, or something."

"Cool. And you get a wheelchair?" Envy infused his voice.

"Yeah. Watch this!" The kid popped a wheelie, balancing on the two large wheels.

"Can I try?"

"Sure." The boy in the wheelchair jumped up and was immediately replaced by the boy with the damaged eye.

What? I had arrived at the infirmary during a surprise emergency drill. Neither of the boys was actually injured. Essentially, I was the only one who actually needed attention. Once the staff realized the emergency wasn't real, they had to proceed as if it was. I waited patiently for hours, completely entertained and absolutely spent. It was the longest I had remained upright since the accident. The staff was processing the last couple of "victims" when a nurse approached me.

"I don't seem to have any paperwork on you."

"Oh, I have my files." I handed her an envelope from the hospital filled with forms and x-rays.

She gasped. "You're a real patient? I thought you were part of the drill."

It was a strange day. I was helped into a bed in a six-patient room. The trapeze was positioned overhead. My legs were propped up on pillows. The call button was nearby, and I went right to sleep. The noise of dinner being delivered woke me. To my surprise, there was a girl about my age sitting at my bedside. She leaned forward when she saw my eyes open.

"Do you think I'm crazy?"

What? "I don't even know you," I managed before a nurse shooed the girl away. Yes, a very strange day.

Life in the Infirmary

Since the infirmary served the campus, the patients were all students. I was the only one in my room with an injury. The other five girls were there because of the emotional stress of being a student. Although I would be spending the rest of the semester there, the other beds constantly hosted new occupants.

College filled me with the excitement of being away from home. I had naively assumed everyone's experience was like mine. However, some of these young women shared their pain, leading me to understand how one-dimensional my view was. It was quite an eye-opener.

Around the time when I felt overwhelmed by the lack of privacy, I became strong enough to sit up without the trapeze. That meant wheels! Graduating to a wheelchair was completely liberating. With wheels under me, I could leave my room on my own. Desperate for some privacy, I found a space where I could hang out almost undetected: the stairwell. I got really good at pulling open the double doors while propelling my chariot through them. I would sit there for hours until someone came by to help me return through the doorway, which did not swing both ways. I loved the isolation.

You would not believe how much weight I lost during my ordeal . . . not that I'm recommending being smashed up in a car as a viable weight loss program. But, as a consumer of the school's unlimited meal plan, I'm pretty sure I hit the proverbial Freshman 10 early first semester, and the second Freshman 10 before the accident. Thanks to the collision, I lost all of that excess weight, and then some. When a couple of my friends helped me sit on an infirmary scale, me, plus fifteen pounds of casts, did not even register 100 pounds. I was so skinny that I could fit my entire arm inside my cast to scratch my knee.

That's why one day I found myself alone in my secluded stairwell, with the weight of my casts tipping my wheelchair forward. Suddenly, I was balancing on the footpads and the small front wheels, suspended over the staircase. Images of my wheelchair crushing me as we tumbled down the stairs kept me frozen in fear, hovering in midair.

I have no idea how long I dangled there. Five minutes? Three hours? It felt like forever until someone came up the stairs and rescued me. Needless to say, the privacy of the stairwell lost its appeal, regardless of how many people crowded into my room.

From Dream to Nightmare

Finally, I was strong enough to do crutches. They traded one of my casts for a walking cast with a lovely knob on the bottom designed to bear weight. My wheelchair was positioned behind a set of parallel bars in the rehab center. The physical therapist instructed me to grip them and stand up. I pulled with my arms, and clenched my torso, and . . . Nothing. "Try again," he encouraged.

I tried again, but in my heart of hearts, I already knew what he didn't. The doctors had missed another problem and I was destined to spend the rest of my life in a wheelchair. Horrorstruck, I fought back tears while going through the motions of trying to get my unresponsive body to stand. I was unsuccessful.

Despair crushed my soul as they wheeled me back to my room. For the next few days, I silently obsessed over my pending role as a paraplegic. How was the doctor going to tell me I was paralyzed from the waist down? How was he going to break the news to my parents? How were my parents going to face me once they knew?

One thing was for sure—I didn't want to spend the rest of my life in a wheelchair. Fully aware that many people led happy, fulfilled wheelchair-bound lives made no difference. This was not the life I had envisioned for myself, so I began to plan my suicide. I had crossed over to the world of my unhappy infirmary roommates. I had my plan all figured out, right down to how to deceive everyone about my intentions. It was the only thing that provided comfort during the private nightmare of those useless rehab appointments.

As I was wheeled back on the third day, I noticed another patient, a UMass football player, sitting in an ice bath. It embarrassed me to have him witness my plight, but I was determined to ignore him and get through the session as quickly as possible. As the only entertainment in the room, the boy watched my halfhearted struggle to stand.

"Hey," he called to the PT after a few pitiful attempts on my part. "Why don't you stand her up and let her sit down? Maybe her body can figure it out backward."

The PT shrugged. "Sure. Why not."

Before I could protest, he grasped me under my arms and hauled me to a standing position. I swayed there for a moment as my life changed forever. I was not going to be permanently wheelchair-bound! I was going to live a normal life! An overwhelming wave of joy and relief washed over me, leaving me weak and trembling. I barely noticed the PT helping me lower back onto the wheelchair.

"I thought I wasn't going to be able to walk again," I managed before I burst into tears. He patted me awkwardly on the arm.

"You shoulda said something. I could've told you wiggling toes and contracting quads means your body still works. It's only atrophied. It just didn't remember how to stand."

"Th-thank you," I sobbed at them both. The football player shrugged and turned pink in the face of my sheer, unrestrained emotion. The pinkened PT shrugged and continued to pat my arm. Guys seem to shrug a lot when they don't know what to say.

"That's enough for today," he decided.

Wonderful. I was completely exhausted. I wheeled to my room, still sobbing, only to find Frank, a friend of mine, waiting. One look at my tear-stained face and he wheeled me back on the elevator. "You need a change of scenery." Frank pushed me off the elevator, through the doors, and into the parking lot where his Volkswagen Beetle waited. Somehow, he got the wheelchair into the back, and we were off.

We didn't talk much after I explained what had transpired. I was too overwhelmed by my good fortune for conversation, and too busy noticing how incredibly blue the sky was; how brightly the sun was shining; how lush and green the scenery was. Everything seemed wonderful.

Several hours later, Frank pulled into a deserted Barnstable beach parking lot on Cape Cod. It was gloriously windy and a bit chilly. He settled me into the wheelchair, wrapped me in a blanket, and wheeled me up the blacktop to where I could see the Atlantic Ocean. Then, Frank gave me the best gift I've ever received. He left me there . . . alone.

Overlooking the beach for about an hour—enveloped in wind, sun, sea and sand—I blossomed inside, vowing to make the most of my splendiferous life. Later, it would also be the impetus for embracing my inner science geek to become a teacher, but for right now, my car accident still wasn't done teaching me *life lessons*.

When It's Not What You Think

Frank was temporarily banned from the infirmary. Apparently, it was against the rules for patients to leave for eight hours and return late in the evening without telling anyone. Who knew? But, hospital rules didn't stop my friends. Since I spent so much time in the stairwell, it was easy for them to sneak me out for a local field trip without being missed.

Where to? *C'mon.* I was a nineteen-year-old girl. Once I learned to use crutches, we went to the mall. What else would I do after losing a lot of weight? I mean, I could see my ribs again! They hadn't been visible since high school. My size 11 clothes definitely were not going to fit me anymore. It was a very exciting time.

My girlfriend and I grabbed an assortment of skirts off the rack to figure out my new size. Then, the oddest thing happened. A size 5 slid off my skinny hips onto the floor. I gleefully snagged a smaller A-line skirt. Pairing the bright knee-length patchwork cotton skirt with a red tank top, I checked out the mirror.

This makes my butt look too big. As I twisted around to verify the size of the skirt, it started to slip down. I hiked it back up and read "2." *What?* How could a size 2 make any body look big in any way?

Despite the loosely - hanging - shirt - draped - over - a - skirt - precariously - perched - on - my - boney - hips reflection, I saw an illusion of a pudgy girl with a size 11 butt. Intellectually, I realized I was too thin, but why couldn't I see it? It was completely baffling. I stared and stared but could not reconcile the mirror's reflection with what my mind saw.

After that, I didn't bother to visit a mall for at least a year. I avoided full-length mirrors because I knew my reflection would not tell me the truth. Instead, my friends shopped for appropriately sized clothes for me and brought them to the hospital to try on. There, I relied on their opinions, instead of my own perception.

Years later, as the young teacher of an anorexic student, I shared this experience with her and her mother to help them understand the illusion the girl saw. Eventually, she recovered, but it was a long and difficult journey for her and her family. Did my words help? I'd like to think so, but definitely the child's resiliency and her family's love deserve most of the credit.

Life Lessons This Incredible Experience Provided

There are far too many life lessons I gleaned from the car accident for me to go into them all, but here's a half dozen of my favorites.

1. I'm an introvert. To be at my best, I need to be alone to recharge. Constant crowds wear me out and don't allow me to refresh, even though I love being around students and their positive energy.

2. Years later, when I shared how I had been planning my suicide, it was suggested those thoughts were produced by depression. I don't know about that. The philosophical desire to maintain a particular quality of life persisted for years, until I became a mom. Once I held that tiny bundle, I knew I'd be fine living in a wheelchair for decades, if it meant I could watch her grow up.

3. I was born to be a science teacher, to infuse the wonders of nature into the academic lives of hundreds of adolescents with laughter and love. I adored nature as a child, but I didn't care for science as a student. The accident opened my eyes, which led me to help others see how everything is connected. I brought my love of the environment and my understanding of teenage angst to the classroom and never looked back. After 27 years, I left teaching to help moms and their teenage daughters navigate their relationship. To this day, the lessons from the accident guide me in my work.

4. First Responders are a unique and incredible group of people. If you know any, please thank them for their service. You wouldn't be reading this if not for them.

5. It was hard to get around in a wheelchair outside of the hospital. Every public building needs inclusively-designed user-friendly accessibility, including adjustments and modifications for entering, exiting, bathrooms, parking, etc. My accident occurred before that was a common practice or federally mandated.

6. To this day, I always hold the door for anyone near me. It's my way of thanking the universe for all the people who helped me in my time of need.

Every day is a gift. If you need to squander a few, that's fine. It's a gift that keeps on giving. I'm happy and proud of the life I've led so far, and excited about the possibilities I haven't yet imagined. I'm so lucky that I realize how lucky I am. Upon hearing about the collision, many people have commented, "You could have died!" I don't agree. Either you die, or you don't. There's no almost to it. The real tragedy would have been going through all that trauma without learning anything. Lucky for me, I learned a lot.

About Deborah Ann Davis

Award-winning author, speaker, and educator, Deborah Ann Davis, B.S., M.Ed., W.I.T.S., founder and member of The Awesome Mom Tribe, has helped countless families navigate the tumultuous teen years, despite the inevitable adolescent angst. As a producer of her own successful teenage daughter, and a former teenager herself, this high school teacher has distilled three decades of experience into exciting live events and insightful books. Her timely information on effective communication, emotional health, and physical well-being provides guidance and encouragement for moms, helping them foster positive and healthy relationships within their families.

After a string of undergrad majors, Deborah realized she could have a captive audience every day in the public school system. As it turns out, teenagers love to laugh, and what could be more entertaining than biology, earth science, and environmental science? Plus, there's the added bonus that once kids know you like to laugh, they want to make you laugh. Go figure.

Deborah happily taught for over 25 years, and somewhere in the middle of all that educating, reunited with and married her childhood sweetheart, twelve years after their first kiss. Thanks to her husband, she was able to pause her teaching career for six years to do the mommy thing for their awesome cherub.

A few years after Deborah's return to the classroom, a tick bit her, introducing a particularly nasty bout of Lyme disease. While recovering, the writing bug bit her and writing eventually replaced her teaching career. However, once everyone returned to school without her that first year, she realized she missed the classroom like crazy.

The solution? Deborah started holding live events for moms and their teenage daughters that provided strategies for navigating their relationship.

They currently reside in lovely Connecticut. On any given day you'll find her:

- writing books that help moms with the motherhood journey
- blogging on any and all topics concerning moms
- creating programs that promote self-worth in teenage girls
- holding live events or online events
- dabbling with living a sustainable life
- dancing, playing outside, and laughing really hard every day

Welcome to Deborah's world. You're going to love what she has to offer.

Deborah Ann Davis
Website (Free copy of *How To Get Your Happy On*): www.deborahanndavis.com
Website (Register for one of Deborah's webinars, seminars, or retreats): www.deborahanndavis.com/events

Keep a lookout for her next book, *How To Keep Your Daughter From Slamming the Door.*

Give Yourself Permission to Be Bold in Your Brilliance

Debbie Belnavis-Brimble

Have you ever been in a crowded room and felt all alone? I have! Even if you haven't had this exact experience, someone in your life probably has, and they suffered in silence. Imagine being in a room with over 100 people and feeling like you are all alone. Imagine feeling out of place, like you don't belong and to top it off, you feel absolutely drained. Throughout my life, I felt this way and didn't realize why. The main reason was that I was protecting myself, or so I thought. I was really protecting those around me from my truth which I believed they couldn't handle. I could never understand why this was the case for me. Until I started to give myself permission to fully embrace who I am and step into the boldness of my brilliance.

My intention as I write this is to support you in *giving yourself the approval to step into your courageous confidence and allow the diamond of your soul to shine brighter than ever before.* When I was younger, I yearned for guidance that I could truly connect with on a deep level. I hope that you find that here as you read my story and the stories of the inspiring women, my sisters and yours.

Beginning

I was always a quiet, reserved child who was always referred to as shy. I would have my moments though when I was the life and soul of the party, always knowing that I had the option of retreating to my solace when needed. I would happily spend hours sitting and playing by myself, with my own thoughts and in my own world. I didn't realize the impact that this would have later on in life. We get our personal cues from our families, teachers, peers, community, culture, and religion. For me, growing up on the beautiful island of Jamaica, I learned to speak when you are spoken to and that children should be seen and not heard. I did all of that, of course, but I was also the rebellious type. I did things when I was ready, including my chores, which wined my mother up something rotten. It wasn't intentional, it was just my way.

I was the kind of child that took things literally. Actually, I still do today as an adult, however, these days I am more in tune with the world and the cues of others. Looking back, there were so many occasions where I felt like I didn't belong, initially because of how I spoke—I spoke with a lisp and was raised to speak *properly*, using the *Queen's English*! My parents met in England where they were married and had their first two daughters before deciding to return to Jamaica where my father's family lived. He was studying in England while my mother had moved there with her parents.

As children, we learn so many lessons; we develop our beliefs, some of our values, and our own family culture very early on. I always felt loved and like I was a part of something amazing with my family. I was surrounded by family, however, at times, I felt like I was misunderstood as a child. This isn't about love, it's a sheer misunderstanding—why did I do things the way I did, why was I interested in other things—I was uniquely me.

At school I didn't have lots of friends, however, the friends that I made were true connections. By the time I got to high school, my sister, who was a few years ahead of me, was involved in Key Club, a student-led organization whose goal is to encourage leadership through serving others. Although I was too young to join, I would sit in on the meetings waiting for my sister, Althea; this was another place where I felt like I belonged. I soon became a member, held a place on the board of directors and then became the youngest president at my school at the time. I have very fond memories of being a part of an organization like that where we were making a significant contribution to the community. We did canned food drives, car washes, various fundraisers, anything we could to raise money for various causes. We collaborated with other high schools and we made an invaluable contribution to society.

I didn't realize at the time, but the reason I felt like I belonged was that I was making a connection with others and a contribution to the world that nourishes my soul. When I am in the presence and energy of like-minded souls, I feel more like myself and at ease. I started to pay attention because I noticed that as I child, I loved my own company because the company of others tended to drain me as I energetically supported others around me who were coping with whatever challenges they had.

Life continued as you would expect, I graduated high school, got my first job at 17 and the signs of not fitting in cropped up again. There were so many occasions during my life where I felt like I just didn't belong. What was it? I analyzed and overanalyzed and read far too much into things, yet it didn't click into place until I got my job in the university where I was studying for my bachelor's degree in computing and business. I loved what I did, supporting others with their computer problems and helping them find a solution.

Realization

This was right up my alley; I love people, I love making connections, I love supporting others and I love making others happy. This was one of those jobs that I thoroughly enjoyed going to. Although there were moments when things were challenging, I realized, I felt like I belonged. Then something changed. I am going to put it down to me: I changed! I suddenly realized that I was becoming like those around me, those that asked daily, "What are you smiling about? Why do you always look so happy?" I felt like I was becoming a clone of negativity.

I started saying things like, "If I don't smile, I will cry." That wasn't me. I was going out socializing with my work colleagues, only to realize,

I just didn't wish to do that, but I was doing it to feel like I belonged. So, I stopped.

That's when things changed. I suddenly realized that I was doing things that were no longer feeding my own soul and warming my heart, I was doing it to fit in and that just didn't feel right to me anymore. Little did I know then, I was going through my rebirth—becoming who I was always meant to be. I could tell that those around me felt uncomfortable, they found it difficult to understand, so they tried to analyze it and come up with all sorts of stories that they wanted to believe. There was talk of me being crazy, ill, unhappy, because there had to be a problem, when in fact this was the solution for the rest of my life. I was spending my days finding solutions for the computer problems that others were experiencing and now, I was spending all my spare time working on the solution to my own soul's calling. I was reconnecting to my purpose, reigniting what I was passionate about, and redefining the possibilities I had available to me.

It's so easy to judge others and believe that they are doing things differently or behaving in a different way. However, what if the person you are judging is standing in their truth and power and the fact that you don't understand their journey causes you to look for reasons that only your consciousness can understand.

My realization was that I wasn't being different, I was embracing my awakening to who I was truly meant to be all along, who I always was, and who I am **becoming**. There is so much power in arriving at that place in your life where you realize that your life is unfulfilled and that you desire so much more than the material things, what you truly desire is more on the inside. After years of searching for happiness on the outside, I started to look deeper within and focused on what truly made my heart sing. It was no longer about supporting the egos of others and making them feel comfortable about their own existence, it was suddenly about me standing in my power and truth and not giving a darn about what others thought about who I was *being*.

I leaned into myself more and listened to my inner child and was reminded of how fulfilled I was when I was making a positive contribution to the lives of others. I felt like I truly belonged to something greater than myself. I was being who I was created to be, living my purpose and sharing my God-given talents with the world.

Purpose

There will always be times along your journey where you think that there must be more to life than this. What am I doing in life? Where am I going? What have I achieved? When you are asking these questions, it is usually because you are at a stage in your life where you are ready! You are ready for the greatest transformation in your life. I became ready at the age of 35. In my work as an Inner Brilliance coach and mentor, I have realized that this seems to be the magic number for many of my clients, the full range is between 32 and 42, in case you are wondering.

At that time in my life, things should have felt magical, yet it didn't always feel that way. I was married to an amazing man following the end of a relationship with the wrong person. You know the type of person who is just a complete mismatch—that was my previous relationship. I am so grateful for the experiences gained as it showed me exactly what I didn't want in the future. I manifested the man of my dreams. I had a great job earning a considerable amount of money, a beautiful home, and yet, I felt incomplete.

I was unhappy with where my life was going, however, I realized that I was surrounded by others who focused on more materialistic things which left me feeling misaligned. This led to me really analyzing the relationships I had and where I focused my energy and with who. I started to realize more and more who I was and that I had amazing gifts to share with the world; just by being in my presence, those who were seeking hope felt amazing about themselves and their lives. I didn't have to do anything, all I had to do was ask the right questions and just listen. This allowed them to hear their own words from their hearts and embrace all that is brilliant about themselves.

I was already on the path to becoming a life coach, supporting others on their journey to tapping into their brilliance, little did I know that the journey would align perfectly to support my own path. As I developed my skills and supported others, my own personal experiences were also shifting. Once you begin your journey of becoming more aligned with your soul's purpose, everything falls into place naturally. Everything feels right as you are presented with the right opportunities, the right people, the right situations, everything begins to align perfectly, as it is meant to. I learned to be open to the possibilities, even those that I didn't expect or even plan.

Decision

It was at that time, I decided that what I was doing wasn't feeding my soul and in fact, I described it as a soul-sucking job. I decided that I no longer had to stay in a role where I was not being fulfilled, rather it was leaving me feeling drained because of all those around me who were feeling out of sync; I was balancing the energy.

I finally decided that I was ready for a new experience after almost 15 years, one of the scariest decisions I could have made, no job to go to, which didn't even concern me. I knew that everything was going to be okay. I even decided to create an even bigger vision. Years previously, I decided to move from England to the United States of America and this was becoming an even more divine time because I was not alone. I had my husband who had embraced this vision more than I had and he wanted to have this new experience.

After making that decision, even more magical experiences started to manifest, like becoming a mother for the first time, attending my first Neuro-Linguistic Programming (NLP) course—again, teaching me invaluable lessons about our mind and how we are programmed from an early age. It introduced me to a new way of thinking which opened my world up even more.

I started to become exposed to a community where they spoke different than the norm, they behaved differently, they responded differently, they did different things and I was in my own heaven. That is where I learned more about who I was and my unique gifts. I was finally home, a place where I knew I belonged.

Acceptance

After years of doing what I believed was expected of me, taking the traditional route, studying, finding a good job, getting married, and starting a family, I finally started to give myself permission to be me in all my authenticity. The people that I started to meet were more spiritual, soulful, and less conventional. This gave me a different perspective of the world, allowing me to see people who were living their life doing what they were passionate about, being unapologetically themselves. This was a very new concept for me as everywhere I looked, I witnessed people from all walks of life just existing, settling with the life they had and forfeiting their true desires.

I started to appreciate all the brilliance that already existed in my life, including those parts of me that I wanted to hide and not fully accept to avoid being judged by others. After all, it was just weird! I started to embrace my weirdness as my unique brilliance. This included my quiet disposition, the fact that I am more of a listener than a talker, feeling drained in large groups as I balance the energy around me, taking time out when I needed to recoup, and so much more. I no longer had to think about what others thought, because I knew that the more I embrace all the brilliance that made me uniquely me, the more beautiful my life was.

Love

I started to notice that with all the transitions that I was experiencing, the greatest impact was as a result of love. Love for oneself, an unconditional kind of love that we all deserve to receive from ourselves. Most of our lives we seek love from external sources, our parents, spouse, children, family, friends, and others. For the first time, I was showering myself with love from myself. I was finally placing myself at the center of my universe.

Sometimes, especially as women, we tend to put our own dreams on hold in order to support the dreams and desires of our loved ones. For me, I was at a place in my life where I decided to finish wearing a mask where I put everyone else first and finally put the person who mattered the most at the center of all that I was doing—me!

Throughout my life, I look back and there were times where I knew I loved the person I was being; however, I didn't love myself unconditionally. What does it really mean to love oneself unconditionally? For me, loving yourself unconditionally is to love yourself in a deep sense with regard, appreciation, and acceptance for who you from a mind, body, spirit, and soul level—no matter what.

Is that you, or has that ever been you? It's not that easy to do, is it? I recall throughout my life, I have been in certain situations where I would bend over backward to support others in their journey, without any regard for myself, my own needs, my own values, or my own dreams and desires. Only to realize that I had been showering others with unconditional love, without any consideration for myself.

The fact that you are reading this book right now, I know that there no doubt has been a time in your own life when this was also your story. You see, you are probably a spouse, a parent, and most definitely a daughter or son, a friend, and so much more to so many. We go through life juggling our many conflicting roles. Pouring of ourselves into the success, nurturing, and love of those around us, yet we neglect ourselves in the process.

I've been the person who was always saying:

"How can I help you?"

"You can count on me."

"Of course, I will help you."

"I'll help in whatever way I can."

"That's my job to help you resolve the issue."

"It's my job to support your goals and vision and your success."

"I will always be there for you."

I have lived my life in service, supporting others, helping them meet their target, achieve their goals and desires, and be successful. I've even carried out all the work and watched someone else claim the glory, but that was okay, or so I told myself. As long as we did a great job and the customers were happy, I was happy.

Have you ever felt like your life was one big revolving door where you lived your life just serving others? I started to feel that way. I was in customer service all my work life. I started my first job at the age of 17 as a customer clerk in a shipping company, often facing happy customers as they received their barrel filled with supplies from abroad—food, clothing, accessories, etc.—and some that were very unhappy with waiting longer than expected to receive theirs.

I was young and although some of the harsh words struck like a knife deep inside, I know that I was doing an amazing job and the happy customers far outweighed the unhappy ones. From an early age, I learned that making others happy was a good thing. When I was growing up on the beautiful island of Jamaica, one of the things that we were taught was to do unto others as you have them do unto you, so I always treated everyone in the same way I wanted them to treat me. That was easy enough, however, I would soon learn that life wasn't like that.

I went about my life as the kind of person who became a doormat. I had to lose myself before I could truly love myself! I was the kind of person who lived my life pleasing everyone else, putting others first, and believing that I was the model of love. I poured love into everyone else, yet the person who truly mattered was staring right back at me in the mirror.

God created me to love unconditionally, even the person who did me wrong; I showered them with love and respect until they burned the bridge of no return. I was raised to do unto others as I would have them do unto me, so even if someone treated me badly, I treated them neutral. I learned to protect myself by developing this skill of disconnecting myself emotionally. It was a great asset in times like ending relationships and friendships which were not real friendships. This was another tool to show me love, by protecting myself.

So how can you love unconditionally when you disconnect from someone? You simply release them from your life to allow yourself to love them from afar. When you are on your journey of truly learning to love yourself, there is sometimes a significant amount of baggage to release and some of those are just there to support your overall well-being.

As well as accepting and embracing who I was, I went even deeper and started to fall madly in love with who I was meant to be, who I was becoming, and chose very carefully who I wanted to be around. I'm talking about falling in love with yourself like when you are in a new relationship and you fall in love with the person you have chosen to be with. That's the kind of love I started to experience for myself. It didn't come overnight; it was a process that took place over a few years.

The process of falling in love with myself was the answer to being truly authentic with who I was and to continue finding the beauty within myself. That inner brilliance, that diamond of your soul that you have buried so deep inside of you, and you protect it fiercely because it is the most precious possession you have ever owned. It is this unique part of you, similar to your fingerprint, only you have this exact combination and design. It includes your purpose, passion, values, courage, confidence, resilience, personality, love, and so much more.

The moment you fall madly in love with yourself is the most magical moment in time. Can you recall a time in life where you truly loved yourself unconditionally? If you are like many, your answer is probably no! Are you ready to make the shift yourself into giving yourself permission to be bold in your brilliance? On your journey to embracing and falling in love with your inner brilliance:

- get to know yourself intimately
- reconnect with who you truly are—know your values, your beliefs, your desires

- create a crystal-clear vision for your future
- understand your inner brilliance by identifying your God-given talents, your purpose, your passion, and know the possibilities that are available to you
- begin to see yourself through a different pair of eyes, the eyes that you use to see others through
- give yourself the love, honor, and respect that you bestow onto others
- cherish every moment that you spend with yourself alone
- create an environment where you are able to display who you truly are
- surround yourself with those who are like you—find your tribe and pour into them as they pour into you
- live every day as if it's your first day on earth, through the eyes of a child who believes in the miracles of Christmas
- look yourself in the mirror every single day and tell yourself why you love yourself unconditionally
- live every day honoring who you are meant to be

When you learn to truly love yourself, you are creating a life where you can achieve everything your heart and soul desire. You are in a position to bring about positive change in your own life and that of others. The minute I started following my heart, the people who were authentic and true to themselves and the world showed up and started to play a significant role in my life; I started to manifest like never before. I had opportunities presented to me that I would never have dreamed of, and of course, all the miracles started to happen. It's time that you too start to show yourself the love that you truly deserve, the kind of unconditional love that allows you to just be who you were created to be. God created a beautiful soul inside of you, a spirit filled with light and magic which was meant to live the life you truly desire, the life you truly deserve. Allow yourself to be submerged into your own inner brilliance today and always remember, you are brilliant, you always have been, and you always will be.

Be bold in your Brilliance!

About Debbie Belnavis-Brimble

Debbie Belnavis-Brimble is the co-founding publisher at Carnelian Moon Publishing, a hybrid publishing agency providing a complete end-to-end service for heart-centered female authors. They believe that everyone has a story to share which will plant seeds of hope around the world.

She has been supporting women (and a few great men) around the world for over 10 years as she accompanies clients on their journey to embracing their true brilliance. As an Inner Brilliance coach and mentor, #1 international bestselling author, NLP master practitioner, Time Line Therapy® provider, a lifelong learner with a master's degree in business administration, wife, and mom, she knows the challenges that so many women face daily dealing with conflicting priorities, especially for those who pour into everyone else's dreams and vision while they sacrifice their own.

Clients who work with Debbie have experienced transformation in their life, career, and business at all levels. Imagine living a life where you finally know your worth, where you begin to know who you truly are and begin to fall madly in love with yourself and have a clear vision of the future.

As the founder of the Inner Brilliance Academy and Debbie Brimble LLC Coaching and Mentoring, she has created programs to support her clients both in person, group programs, one-on-one programs, as well as online, including her signature program, *Embrace Your True Brilliance.*

Her core belief is that we all entered this world as brilliant beings and we tend to bury our brilliance deep within our core, similar to diamonds deep within the earth's core. Her work is likened to the volcanic pipes that push the diamonds to the surface of the earth. Debbie reminds her clients of the brilliance that they innately possess and teaches them to embrace their brilliance and give themselves permission to shine brighter than ever before.

While accompanying her clients on their journey as they decide to live a fulfilling life of purpose with passion and appreciating the infinite possibilities available to them, her processes support her clients in knowing themselves intimately, defining and designing their life for ultimate success with ease and joy.

Debbie understands the many roles juggled by women, such as being a wife/partner, mother, daughter, granddaughter, sister, friend, and so much more to so many; life can take its toll as everyone else has priority. Her programs have been designed to give back to ourselves unapologetically because we deserve all that we desire and then some!

Reconnecting with one's inner power, creativity, and resourcefulness, doing what we are passionate about, doing something that we love and something that is in alignment with our values is real living. It's time to change the world by changing how we as women see ourselves daily and start loving who we are, in all our brilliance by identifying our gifts, formulating a blueprint to successes, and initiating our inner resources. It's time to take back full control of our lives and be our most authentic selves!

Download your free guide to support you in becoming an author today at carnelianmoonpublishing.com.

Sign up for your free online program—*Be Empowered by Your Brilliance* at innerbrillianceacademy.com.

Debbie's Coaching and Publishing

Website (Coaching & Mentoring): www.innerbrillianceacademy.com

Website (Publishing): www.carnelianmoonpublishing.com

This page is intentionally left blank

Your Choice

Eight women came together and shared their stories, their experiences, their wisdom, and their truth to support you in gaining hope and knowing that you too have a choice to step into your inner brilliance. It is so easy to fall into a place where darkness resides, imagine having a choice to be on the brilliant side where you know who you are, you know your worth, you are connected to your confidence deep within, and you are madly in love with who you are meant to be.

Wherever you are in your journey right now, know that you have the power of choice and it is time.

Time to take your power back.

Time to choose you.

Time to know what you truly desire in your life.

Time to choose your desires.

Time to identify your goals.

Time to focus on your goals.

Time to step into who you are truly meant to be.

Time to live your purpose.

Time to do what you are passionate about.

Time to reconnect to what makes you brilliant.

Time to fully accept your gifts.

Time to fully embrace your true brilliance.

Time to be boldly you.

Time to be boldly brilliant.

It is time to choose you.

The co-authors of this book thank you for giving yourself the gift of hope, inspiration, and empowerment by reading these words and invite you to continue your journey with us if our services or stories resonate with you through our directory.

Continue your journey of knowing the *Power of Your Inner Brilliance* through igniting your self-love, self-worth, and inner confidence.

Directory of Brilliance: Connect With Our Authors

Winifred Adams
Making Life Brighter
United States of America
www.makinglifebrighter.com

Laura Atyeo
Open Harmony
United Kingdom
www.openharmony.co.uk

Debbie Belnavis-Brimble
Carnelian Moon Publishing &
Inner Brilliance Academy
United Kingdom and United States of America
www.carnelianmoonpublishing.com
www.innerbrillianceacademy.com

Isha B. Campbell
Donna Marie Foundation
United States of America and Jamaica
www.donnamariefoundation.com

Deborah Ann Davis
Deborah Ann Davis
United States of America
www.deborahanndavis.com

Angelique Miralles
E-Motion Deep & Coaching Leadership
France
www.coaching-leadership.net
www.e-motiondeep.com

Judith Richardson Schroeder
Carnelian Moon Publishing & Guidance from Within
Canada
www.carnelianmoonpublishing.com
www.guidancefromwithincoaching.com

Janet Wiszowaty
Worldly Connektions
Canada
www.familyconnekt.com

CPSIA information can be obtained
at www.ICGtesting.com
Printed in the USA
LVHW040606030320
648785LV00004B/14